A Survival Guide
for Paralegals

The West Legal Studies

Your options keep growing with West Legal Studies

Each year our list continues to offer you more options for every area of the law to meet your course or on-the-job reference requirements. We now have over 140 titles from which to choose in the following areas:

Accounting and Financials for the Law Office
Administrative Law
Alternative Dispute Resolution
Bankruptcy
Business Organizations/Corporations
Civil Litigation and Procedure
CLA Exam Preparation
Computer in the Law Office
Contract Law
Criminal Law and Procedure
Document Preparation
Elder Law
Employment Law
Environmental Law
Ethics
Evidence Law
Family Law

Intellectual Property
Interviewing and Investigation
Introduction to Law
Introduction to Paralegalism
Law Office Management
Law Office Procedures
Legal Nurse Consulting
Legal Research, Writing, and Analysis
Legal Terminology
Paralegal Employment
Product Liability
Real Estate Law
Reference Materials
Social Security
Sports Law
Torts and Personal Injury Law
Will, Trusts, and Estate Administration

You will find unparalleled, practical support

Each book is augmented by instructor and student supplements to ensure the best learning experience possible. We also offer custom publishing and other benefits such as West's Student Achievement Award. In addition, our sales representatives are ready to provide you with dependable service.

We want to hear from you

Our best contributions for improving the quality of our books and instructional materials is feedback from the people who use them. If you have a question, concern, or observation about any of our materials, or you have a product proposal or manuscript, we want to hear from you. Please contact your local representative or write us at the following address:

West Legal Studies, 5 Maxwell Drive, Clifton Park, NY 12065-2919

For additional information point your browser at

www.WestLegalStudies.com

Contents

Acknowledgments

The authors and Delmar Learning would like to express their gratitude to the professionals, named below, who offered numerous, valuable suggestions, as well as to the many paralegals who agreed to speak with us on condition of anonymity. Thank you to:

Valerie Chaffin, Patty Dietz-Selke, Lori Gray, Kimberly M. Hill, Patti Huggins, Marie Micheli, Dina Newton, Cheryl K. Sheppard, Deborah L. Sherk, Barb Villani, Kathy Wrobel, and Annie Yanez. We would also like to thank Janice Hoover for her help with this book.

CHAPTER 1

The Paralegal Life

Most people in the world have an ambivalent relationship with their work. Sometimes the need to work can seem like one of life's unfortunate complications. Other times, work becomes a renewable, self-sustaining source of energy, pleasure, and self-esteem. Few of us out there in the work world spend time exclusively at either one end or the other of the continuum. Most of us travel up and down the line, some days in the bad zone but, hopefully, most days in a far more rewarding place of job satisfaction.

Paralegals, like everyone else in the work world, have their good days and their bad days, enjoying some aspects of the job while finding other tasks dull or onerous. In the course of writing this book, we spoke with a great many paralegals who shared their feelings about their work. For the most part, the people we spoke with felt gratified to be in a field where they could use their minds productively, be regarded as an important part of a professional team, and claim a set of skills that would always make them employable. This book brings together the trade secrets of your fellow paralegals that have helped them perform more effectively in their jobs. You will read tips on everything from personal grooming to how to handle an interview, from ways to protect the information on your hard drive to strategies for dealing with a forgetful boss, from asserting yourself when you're being taken advantage of to finding ways to relax and recharge while sitting in your desk chair. There are hundreds of tips to digest and cumulatively they will lead you toward more fulfillment, healthier ways of coping, and a better balance between your work life and your personal life.

PARALEGALS DEFINED

Just in case this book falls into the hands of people who are not paralegals, but who may be on their way to becoming paralegals or perhaps are just in the stage of thinking that they might someday want to become a paralegal, it would be good to make sure we are all on the same page, as it were, when it comes to job definitions. Simply put, a paralegal, also known as a *legal assistant,* is a person who is sufficiently trained in the law to be able to assist attorneys with the delivery of legal services.

As a paralegal, you may encounter some confusion in the public mind about what exactly it is that you do. Inform your friends that legal assistants work directly under the supervision of attorneys. That said, there are some paralegals—those who refer to themselves as "independent paralegals" or "legal technicians"—who work autonomously to provide certain legal services directly to the public, such as obtaining and/or filing legal forms. It is imperative, however, that all paralegals realize that there are functions they are not allowed to perform. Paralegals cannot give legal advice; they cannot set legal fees; and they cannot (with rare exceptions) represent a client in court. On the other hand, there are so many functions that a paralegal *can* perform, including the following:

- Drafting legal documents
- Keeping a legal calendar and tracking deadlines for filing purposes
- Assisting attorneys in preparing for trials
- Interviewing clients and witnesses
- Conducting legal investigations and gathering facts through the perusal of medical records, police reports, and other such documents
- Organizing and maintaining client files
- Conducting legal research

Although these are just some of the vital functions that lie within the province of the paralegal, they suggest why the paralegal field is so fast-growing. In this day and age of soaring legal costs, paralegals can do much of the work of attorneys, thereby making reduced legal costs a possibility for the consumer.

The scope of the paralegal's duties and activities varies widely from one setting to another. In a one-lawyer office, a paralegal will most likely perform a range of tasks that, in a larger firm, would be taken on by a support staff of receptionists, secretaries, and clerical workers. In a small office, the paralegal might be asked to do photocopying or to cover the phones while the secretary is out to lunch. There is no indignity attached to such requests, and many paralegals prefer the intimacy of such an environment. Other paralegals choose to work in a corporate setting with in-house counsel on assignments that might include any or all of the following: scheduling corporate meetings;

drafting meeting notices, agendas, and minutes; preparing case files; collecting and interpreting technical information for corporate reports to government agencies; drafting documents necessary for patents, trademarks, or copyright protection; or researching laws and regulations that could affect the formulation of corporate policies or that might influence corporate actions. About 20 percent of all paralegals work for corporations and, for the most part, they enjoy higher wages than non-corporate paralegals, as well as more regular hours and less stress as a result of not having to amass billable hours.

One of the "perks" of being a paralegal, as attested to by professionals such as yourself, is the enormous variety and versatility built into the field. Paralegals work in the fields of employment law, bankruptcy law, intellectual property law, immigration law, family law, real estate law, environmental law, probate law, criminal law, elder law, and more. There are many paralegals who start in one area and move around to other areas until they find the right "fit." But no matter where you ultimately land, as a paralegal you will be called upon to utilize skills in the following four basic areas:

- **Organizational skills**—Part of a paralegal's job is to help organize the activities and the calendars of attorneys. An inability to think in an organized way would be a serious handicap for anyone pursuing this vocational direction.

- **Analytical skills**—Inevitably, you will encounter certain routine aspects in your work as a paralegal, but, thankfully, these less exciting aspects are compensated for by the emphasis placed on exploring complex theories, facts, and patterns. Part of your job will be to take these complex units and to break them down into smaller, more easily understood components, both for your own benefit and to assist the supervising attorney with whom you are working. You will also be synthesizing material—putting together facts and legal concepts to "paint a picture," whether it is from a client you are interviewing, a witness, or whomever.

- **Computer skills**—These days, the world of the paralegal is thoroughly enmeshed with the world of advanced computer technology. This technology has utterly transformed the field of law and your ability to stay technologically abreast may be a major determinant in how others assess your worth.

- **Interpersonal skills**—As with any job in which you have day-to-day interactions with other people, your performance will be judged, in large part, on the success with which you deal with others. Are you a team player? Can you handle criticism? Do people like you and do you like people? These are vital questions to ask yourself.

One of our objectives in writing this book was to amass tips from successful paralegal professionals working in every kind of employment setting and to pass those tips on to you so that you could improve your performance in the four critical areas mentioned above. The good news is that most of us can make significant strides in these areas if we concentrate, listen, work hard, and stay open to the feedback of others. You deserve to be congratulated. You have come far, doing important work that impacts on peoples' lives; you are making a very respectable income; and you are feeling good about your accomplishments. But it is useful to remember that, as a paralegal, you will always need to keep learning, to continue your education, and to be the best you can be. You owe this to others and you owe it to yourself.

PARALEGALS: PERSPECTIVES ON THE PROFESSION

As we indicated above, most of us in the work world suffer our agonies and our ecstasies. In the world of paralegals, there are big challenges but lots of payoffs. Let's hear what some of your fellow paralegals have to say about the pros and cons of the field.

❖ The thing I like best about my work is the creativity. I started out in life as a graphic artist, but I couldn't make a go of it. When I decided to become a paralegal, I thought I'd have to permanently put creativity on the back-burner. But that hasn't been the case at all. The kind of thinking you have to use in this field is very creative in nature. It's not just memorizing or following some prescribed routine. Whether you're researching or writing an argument or drafting a pleading or coming up with questions to ask a witness, it's all about using your mind in a fresh way, every day. To me, that's creative.

❖ I think the worst thing in life is being bored, but, ultimately, being bored is just a choice that some people make. Even jobs we think of as boring can be interesting depending on the depth you bring to the pursuit. Certainly, as a paralegal, boredom is not something I ever have to worry about. The law is constantly changing, day to day. If you don't keep up, you can't do the job you're meant to do. So with that kind of challenge, how could anyone be bored?

❖ I'm a freelance paralegal, so not only do I feel fueled by the intellectual task of knowing the law, but I've developed and gotten to use a whole set of business skills I never expected to acquire. I have to think about marketing, planning, accounting. To me, that's half the fun!

❖ The fantastic thing about working as a paralegal is that you are involved, in a meaningful, ongoing way, with the law, and law is really all about human nature. That's why you've got your retirees who pass their day sitting in courtrooms watching trials. It's better than anything you'll find on TV. And I'm not just talking about criminal law. All of law is about human nature, the struggle between people, right and wrong. There's so much drama even in a minor tort case. It's incredible how much I've learned about human nature since I became a paralegal and how much I apply that knowledge to all the other areas of my life when I deal with people.

❖ The research turns me on. I used to think I wanted to be a journalist, and now I feel like I am, sort of. It's like I'm Encyclopedia Brown or something. I'm given a problem to solve, and off I go. To know how to get what you need by using the incredible resources available to you creates a real feeling of empowerment.

❖ I love my work, but it's got its challenges. For one thing, working for an attorney is not like working for a golf pro. Attorneys are, for the most part, very intense, pressured people who are apt to make a lot of demands on their staff. If you can't stand the heat, this kitchen's not going to be for you. And then when you get past the attorneys, you have the clients, who can be even more of a challenge.

❖ I really enjoy the camaraderie and community that comes from being part of a team. And it's not just with the attorney I work for and the other people in my office. I feel a real sense of connection to all the people I know and deal with, in the doctors' offices, the judges' offices, the insurance adjusters and examiners, the court clerks. There are a lot of people in my life that I have a lot of respect for, and that feels good.

❖ I'm in Legal Services and a hard part of the job for me was to learn how to handle all the emotions that get scratched up by the clients I work with. People would come in and tell me incredible stories of loss and adversity and there would go my day, down the chute. Now I know that when you're involved in the field of law, you have to build up a reserve of objectivity and resistance, just as you do in the field of medicine.

❖ My greatest challenge is staying on top of schedules. The attorney I work for is incredibly bright, but she's also incredibly overloaded and the amount of juggling I have to do sometimes makes me feel like I should be in Ringling Brothers Barnum & Bailey Circus instead of a law office. Sometimes, when the acid's pouring into my stomach by around mid-day, I fantasize about what it must be like to work in a sane environment, if there is such a thing.

❖ The worst thing about being a paralegal? The continuing education you have to factor into your life. The best thing about being a paralegal? The continuing education you have to factor into your life. I have a love-hate relationship with continuing education, because sometimes the idea of going to another seminar or workshop just exhausts me. But then, when I get there, I'm usually really turned on by learning something new and I have no idea what I was complaining about in the first place.

As we said at the beginning of this chapter, and as the preceding comments of your peers testify, paralegal work is filled with many opportunities for satisfaction and ample opportunities for overload and frustration. How can men and women working in the paralegal profession hold on to the good feelings while dealing effectively with the drawbacks and negative feelings? For starters, they can learn from each other. No one is better equipped to offer support and advice to paralegals than other paralegals who are out there, in the field, discovering on a day-to-day basis what works and what does not.

This book is a compilation of hints, tips, and advice from paralegals all over the country. As writers, we gathered this information and then organized it in a way that we thought would be useful, but we never tampered with the information. We are not paralegal experts. We are the channel through which you will hear from the experts.

The nitty-gritty advice in this book, however, needs to be placed in the context of broader, more sweeping principles. We have developed these principles during the course of writing Survival Guides for professionals in a number of different fields. These Seven Principles that you are about to learn are designed to help you determine what you value most in your life and how you can make room for these things you most value. When you start to get a perspective on these issues, life in general, and your work life in particular, become far more rewarding.

SEVEN GUIDING PRINCIPLES

Once you have read through these principles, it is important to do what you can to keep them firmly in mind. You can post them on the wall by your desk or keep them in your wallet or have them on an index card in your bag. If you want, you can turn them into a poem or a song and chant them at quiet times or once a day in the morning or before you go to sleep. The goal is to develop a healthy perspective that will sustain you over the long run, that will enable you to have fun and enjoy life, and that will help you remember, at the end of a day, what it is that you love about your work.

Principle #1: Become an Active Listener

It is a given that if you have found yourself in the paralegal field, you have learned to become a listener. A person could not survive in this field without knowing how to listen, because a large part of your job has to do with following instructions. In any event, we can all do with a refresher course when it comes to listening and elsewhere in this book you will find specific tips on techniques like reflective listening, in which you reinforce what a person says by returning their questions and comments to them. As a guiding principle, however, we stress the importance of taking the time in a busy day to listen to others and to really hear what they have to say. Many of us are so overwhelmed by the demands and stresses of our work and personal lives that we look for relief by drowning out our surrounding environment. In fact, this drowning-out process intensifies stress. You can relieve stress better by keeping open the lines of communication and enjoying the contact and camaraderie that is always possible in your relationships with staff and clients. Keep in mind, however, that by communication we do not mean idle gossip or pointless chitchat. By communication, we mean the act of engaging with others in real dialogue—saying what you have to say and actively listening to what comes back to you.

Principle #2: Thinking Outside the Box

Life will be a lot more satisfying if you avoid the trap of conventional, unimaginative, stereotyped thinking. As we said, being a paralegal involves performing certain tasks that are highly routinized, but the most important aspects of your job involve analytical and creative thinking. You need to find ways to keep your mind alive and fresh outside of your job and outside of the box. Thinking outside the box will also help you to avoid stereotypical thinking that will get in your way as a paralegal. Preconceptions about people are routinely dashed when you see them in a legal context and trying to hold on to these preconceptions can lead to trouble. Having an expansive, long-range view of things is a good way of thinking outside the box. You may feel stuck in a rut right now, but you need to keep your dreams alive and know that life is always filled with surprises that might take you to places you never even imagined.

Principle #3: Take Time to Figure Out What You Find Most Satisfying

Well-organized systems and routines can help ensure smooth sailing for paralegals such as yourself, but routines can be overdone as well. When this happens, you may begin to feel like a robot, moving through your day without really thinking about what you're doing.

Mihaly Cziksentmihalyi, Ph.D., Professor of Psychology at the Drucker School of Management at Clermont Graduate University, did a study with adolescents where he outfitted them with beepers that went off eight times a day over the course of one week each year. Every time the beeper signaled, the subjects would report in to Dr. Cziksentmihalyi about what they were doing and how they were feeling about it. Among other things, Dr. Cziksentmihalyi found that when people are involved in an activity they enjoy, they develop a sense of *flow*, a great feeling of energy that makes them want to continue doing what they're doing and return to it whenever possible.

In Chapter 2, we will offer a tool and a technique to help you figure out just which activities give you a sense of flow. We will help you assess how you spend your time and how you feel about what you're doing. We will take you through your day—before, after, and during work—and analyze where you feel most and least satisfied. This kind of honest assessment is a critical step you need to take before moving on to Principle #4.

Principle #4: Create Time for the Things You Care About

The idea of shifting your time and energies to accommodate the things you most enjoy may seem like common sense, but you would be surprised how few people actually live by this principle. Too many of us carry around a "can't do" attitude when it comes to changing our patterns. The good news is that most of us "can do" this kind of alteration.

Suppose you discover that you feel most ready to meet your workday after you have had thirty minutes of quiet time to sit, read the paper, and sip your coffee. Or perhaps you can achieve a better mood for the day if you've been able to take a walk before work begins. You may learn that by shifting morning chores with your spouse and children, you can free up the time you need. Or you might decide to set your alarm a half-hour earlier every day.

With regard to work, you may have systems in place, but are you maximizing your efficiency and enjoyment? The key is to begin thinking about how you can best meet your needs, because when your needs are met, you will be better equipped to meet the needs of others.

Principle #5: Learn to Enjoy What's in Front of You

There is a Buddhist practice called "mindfulness" that teaches the value of focusing on what is beautiful in the here and now. Mindfulness advocates living in the moment, and learning to develop this kind of vision is a huge help in clearing away the clutter in our lives.

How often have you found yourself thinking about everything other than what you are doing? You might be sitting in a staff meeting and your mind is wandering to your bills, that worrisome school conference you had about your kid, the bad wheezy sound coming out of your car (or you!), or a million other things. Think about what it would be like to really focus in on the moment and to be getting the most out of that meeting. Your colleagues and boss are all smart people who have a lot of worthwhile things to say. *You* have a lot of worthwhile things to say, too, and your active participation will go a long way toward making your office a better environment.

This practice of mindfulness can and should be used outside of work too. When you are driving home, for instance, instead of thinking about your bills/worrisome school conference/weird sound in the car, think instead about how beautiful the light in the sky looks at that very moment or how peaceful the sound of the rain on your rooftop is.

Principle #6: Learn to Be Flexible

There is no such thing as a day that goes exactly according to plan. You have to learn to roll with the punches and the bumps and the trap doors that are always opening up all over the place. Law is a field particularly filled with the unexpected. No two days are the same. Deadlines breathe down your neck only to get changed at the last minute.

Some people take change hard and think that they can get around it by setting down ironclad "rules" that others must follow. Such people are often perceived by others as difficult, temperamental, *inflexible* sorts who do not inspire affection or loyalty.

If you think of yourself as a kind of machine that is out there every day getting the job done (but of course you are much more than that!), then flexibility is the lubricant that keeps your gears in working order. Stress is vanquished in the face of flexibility and flexibility also softens the hard edges that can often be present in one's interactions with others. Flexibility will keep you from turning into a tight rubber band, ready to snap. It serves as a strong and pliable elastic that allows you to retain your shape.

Principle #7: Prioritize

Once you know what you have to do, and what you *love* to do, it's time to prioritize and to get rid of all the unnecessary, energy-sapping tasks that you dread. You'll be shocked by just how much choice you have about where to invest your efforts. Remember to keep track of what you actually do with your time. Ask yourself the following:

- What do I need to do to take care of myself that absolutely no one else can do? For example, do I need to meditate at the end of a long day after having dealt with the needs of other people? Or do I need to make dinner plans with others from the office to cement my working relationships with them?
- Which of my responsibilities can I put off for the moment with no harm done? For example, can I take care of some correspondence at home? Can I come in early tomorrow and proofread that document instead of trying to do it on this crazy day?
- What am I doing that someone else could be doing for me? Am I making full use of others in the office and out of the office?

Embodying these Seven Guiding Principles is not a process that happens overnight. Some people take months, even years, before they can internalize them, and, even then, most of us have to be vigilant about not letting our counterproductive habits creep back into control. But we are not putting these principles forth as way to create even more pressure for you. As time goes on, these principles will come to feel like second nature and, when you fully understand them and live by them, you will appreciate and enjoy a quality of life you might never have experienced otherwise.

War Stories:
An Overview

When it comes down to it, the big issue in the life of most paralegals is the kind of supervising attorney that one is assigned. Here are examples from a paralegal who has made a study of the personalities—or shall we say, the personality problems—of the attorneys she has worked with:

I. The Alcoholic

The Problem: The man had a drinking problem . . . a very serious one. He would claim he told me to do something when he never did. Sometimes he'd yell at me for doing something he never remembered he asked me to do.

The Response: Since he was right, no matter what, I played the ditz-ball and told him that in order for me to keep my act straight, he would need to put every assignment in a written memo to me. (At that time, there was no such thing yet as e-mail). After he was confronted with his written words a few times, he stopped pestering me . . . but never stopped drinking!

II. The Psychotic

The Problem: I had two such psychotics—both women and both with many self-esteem and ego issues. They were Dr. Jekyll one moment, Ms. Hyde the next. Or, otherwise put, coherent one second, shrill and raving the next.

The Response: At the time, I had enough stamina to be a "girlfriend" to each of them. However, the sanity that this can bring to the situation in one moment can mushroom into psychosis for both of you if you don't watch out. I don't recommend this response, unless you have a background in social work or counseling.

III. The Absent-Minded Professor

The Problem: His office was a mess. He always missed deadlines, left and right. He lost everything, constantly.

The Response: We gave him false deadlines two or three days ahead in order to make sure he'd meet the actual deadlines. These types of attorneys (many of whom, I have to say, are elderly) are very, very appreciative of someone who can organize their files and their schedules. In the end, working for attorneys like this can be rewarding, because they know they can't handle their workload without you and they aren't afraid to say so.

CHAPTER 2

Staying on Track

Generally, when people ask, "How are you doing?" we answer, "Fine. Thank you." That is just the way it is. We do not really expect people to be interested in what was bad or good about our day. But in that typical exchange—*"How are you doing?" "Fine. Thank you"*—something often gets lost. The details of our day tend to merge and become one big blur. In allowing that to happen, we run the risk of becoming almost as uninterested and inattentive to what is going on in our lives as those people who keep asking us that same hollow question.

In this book, we suggest that you start giving some serious thought to how you spend your day. The best way to begin to do this is by keeping a record of where your time goes. Most of us are awake and active sixteen out of every 24 hours. (That is on a good day. Unfortunately, for some of us the waking day stretches out to 18 or 19 hours). In those waking hours, some of what we do makes us feel great. We are kept busy with things that leave us feeling energized and happy, surfing along with that sense of "flow" we cited in the first chapter. But, unfortunately, all of us have to spend some of those waking hours involved in activities that we would rather not be doing, engaged in pursuits that are boring or unpleasant or that we even dread.

In many instances, we just do not have much choice about what we have to do. With rare exceptions, most people are faced with the need to attend to some of the humdrum activities of life. Paying bills, doing the laundry, going grocery shopping—sometimes it all feels so relentless and laborious. But it is our belief that most of us actually have more control over our lives than we give ourselves credit for. The key is to begin to think about what it is that we do with our time and to keep track of our feelings with regard to these activities. Once we have done that, we can begin to think about making changes.

This book focuses on how to simplify and improve the professional lives of paralegals. To that end, however, it is important that you explore the ways in which you spend your time not only at work, but also before and after work. There is a direct emotional link from one sphere of your life to the other.

One paralegal we spoke with, Elaine, worked in Boston in a practice that specialized in immigration law. Her job involved dealing with frequent emergencies and attending to the needs of desperate clients and their families. Elaine told us how she'd gotten into this habit of coming home from work every night, fixing dinner for her family, and then collapsing in front of whatever was on TV. "And I'm not even talking about *Law and Order* or something that might have some meaning for me," she said. "I'd sit there for hours just watching *Wheel of Fortune* and *Biography* shows about people I didn't even care about. I was so overtired that all I wanted to do was veg out."

A friend of Elaine's persuaded her to take a pottery class at a local community college. "My friend and I go back to high school," Elaine said. "She knew me back in the '70s when I was making macramé and batik and all that and loving it. And she was right. Just having my hands in clay again was the most therapeutic thing imaginable. It was the perfect antidote to the constant head work I have to do at the office."

The class was a revelation for Elaine, for whom the idea of going out at night during the week had been unimaginable. "I lived for that class," she said. "Thursdays would come and I wouldn't even go home. I'd go out for pizza with my girlfriend and let my daughter, who's 16, take care of dinner at home. Doing this for myself made such a difference. I felt more energized than I had for ages, and that renewed energy spilled over into my worklife too. I was better on the job—fresher, more responsive, better able to cope."

Elaine came to realize that when you spend your days attending to the needs of other people, you often run out of juice when it comes to taking care of your own needs. It is crucial to make time for your spouse or partner, your children, your extended family, your friends, and, last but hardly least, yourself. You need to set aside time to cultivate your outside interests, your hobbies, and all those facets that go into making you a multi-faceted person.

This is not to say that there is anything wrong with vegging out in front of the TV when you feel like it. There is a time and a place for everything and our purpose in this book is not to pass judgment or set down rules. If *Wheel of Fortune* is your speed at any given moment, then go with it. But if Pat Sajak and Vanna White are somehow making you feel even more tired and drained—if all that TV-watching actually saps you of your energy, as such passive activity can tend to do—then it is time to find another kind of release.

Figure 2-1 Daily Activity Chart

	Activity #1	Activity #2	Activity #3
START			
STOP			
TOTAL			
FEELINGS			
EFFICIENCY			
WHAT'S MY ROLE			

KEEPING TRACK

In order to develop an awareness of how you feel about the way you are spending your time, you need to do some work. Fortunately, the personality profiles of most paralegals suggest that this is just the kind of work they like to do. The pages that follow in this chapter make up a workbook of sorts. Look at the column headings in Figure 2–1. Copy them into a notebook that you can carry with you throughout the day. A small spiral-bound pad will fit into almost any coat or jacket pocket for easy access.

Ideally, you will be creating a journal or log that reflects exactly what you do with your time in the course of any given day. This technique works especially well if you stay at it for a full week. Keeping track of your weekend activities and the feelings they engender can provide an interesting contrast to the study of your work-week habits.

It may be difficult for you to take the few minutes necessary to log activities. When you've got contracts that need drafting or clients waiting to be interviewed, it is not easy to find the time to make notes about your feelings. Just do the best you can to jot down the notes while the experience is still fresh. If you can glance at your watch and make a mental note of the time you begin and end an activity, you can always jot it down later.

Some people find it easier to make notes on a tape recorder or dictation machine. Do whatever works for you, and do it as well as you can. The idea is not to create another burden in your life, but to help you develop a powerful sense of awareness regarding the way you spend your time.

Let us have a look at the categories you will be keeping track of.

Start/Stop/Total

In this phase of taking stock, you will need to be conscious of the clock, right from the moment your alarm goes off in the morning until you close your eyes at night. Think about the distinct areas into which your activities fall: scheduling; drafting documents; calling around to other offices to collect information; organizing and maintaining client files; doing research; and so on. Check the clock when you begin one new activity and jot down the time. Do the same when you finish that activity and before you move on to the next one. Do not neglect to factor in things like "conferencing with staff" and the like. Just a few minutes spent with a colleague discussing a case should be factored into your log. Whatever you do, do not worry about the "total time spent" until later. You do not need to burden yourself with adding, subtracting, and justifying yourself in the middle of a busy day.

Activity

This is where you will note what category your activity falls into. The more specific you are, the more you will learn from this log at the end of the week. Everything that is a part of your day should find its way into your log. And remember, this is not something you will be graded on. You are the sole creator, contributor, and judge of what is included, and you are the only one who will be reading it. The goal is to learn about yourself—how you spend your time and how you feel about yourself during the course of a day.

Paralegals work in a high-stress job. Many demands are made on them and the work can be psychologically, emotionally, and even physically taxing. Maintaining this log should never feel like an additional burden. The goal is to make your life easier, and despite the extra effort this will require, for a short period at least, it will ultimately go a long way toward meeting that goal. Hang in there and do the best that you can with it.

Feelings

Try to jot down your feelings soon after you have finished an activity. The closer you are to the feelings, the less likely you will be to edit them, either consciously or unconsciously. Keep in mind that you do not need to write long, detailed notes here. A few words, if well chosen, will do fine. Begin by thinking in terms of "feeling" words: happy, sad, angry, bored, worried. More clarification might come by thinking in terms of opposites —happy/sad; relaxed/tense; worried/optimistic; loving/angry; gentle/tough; energetic/tired; interested/bored—and seeing which of the two poles in each instance you are feeling closer to.

It is also important in this section to gauge how much satisfaction you are getting out of your activities. Most of us have to do things that are not necessarily fun, but aspects of these activities can still give us a deep sense of satisfaction. If you are the sort of person who has always gotten a thrill out of lining drawers with shelf paper, then you probably really enjoy the organizational aspect of your job. If you're a "people" person, you might enjoy the client contact the most. If you always prided yourself on what a good student you were, chances are you look forward to the research aspect of your work

Once you figure out what it is that gives you pleasure and a sense of well-being, you will be in a better position to think about how you can adjust things to make the most of those activities and make the least of the ones you do not find satisfying. Perhaps you can create new, streamlined systems to get you through the onerous part of the day more quickly. Maybe you can swap certain tasks with someone else in the office who likes what you hate and vice versa. Creative thinking is the buzzword here, but, again, remember not to think too hard and too long when you write down your reactions. Your gut response is probably the most reliable. Again, keep in mind that this log is for your eyes only. Do not worry about what others will think of you when you put down your honest reactions. This log is a tool that exists only to make your life simpler and more pleasant. As we said previously, it is not something you are going to be graded on.

Efficiency

Overall, paralegals are efficient people. This is their stock in trade. But keep in mind that efficiency is not necessarily the highest ideal in the world. We have all known people who are incredibly efficient and who bore us to tears. There are even derogatory names for people like that: *nitpicker* and *bean-counter* come to mind. On the other hand, people who put efficiency on the back burner have a whole other list of insulting nicknames to choose from, including *flake, airhead,* and *scatterbrain.* Where do you fall? Do you freak out if your pencils aren't lined up like little toy soldiers? If someone moves something of yours, do you turn on the siren and put out an all-points bulletin? Or are you a secretly sloppy person? Is your desk immaculate but does your bag bulge at the seams with equal weight given to important things, like a client's business card, and things that are trivial, like an expired coupon to a car wash in a neighborhood you almost never get to? The point of the log is to look at the matter of efficiency— how best to use your time—and to strike a balance that is comfortable for you and the people you work with and live with.

There will be many instances in the log where efficiency really is not all that relevant. For example, if you are looking at the time of day when you cook dinner, you may find that you do not necessarily choose to be as efficient as possible. While you might have a food processor that could do the job of chopping vegetables much faster than you can by hand, perhaps on that particular evening you are deriving a certain contemplative comfort from doing the task by hand, enjoying the feel of the vegetables and the steady slice of the knife. Maybe that is just the medicine you need to bring you down from a stressful day. So if efficiency does not apply to a given task, simply write NA (not applicable) in your log. Otherwise, make an effort to rate your efficiency in any given activity on a 1-to-5 scale.

Role

In the three-act play called *A Day In Your Life,* you play a host of roles over the course of 24 hours. You may be parent, child, spouse, partner, manager, confidante, taskmaster, mentor, confessor, social worker . . . you name it. It is useful to think about which roles you most enjoy, and which suit you best. Compile a list, somewhere in the back of your notebook or pad, of all the roles you play over the course of a given week. Use it as a reference when you make your log entries.

When you get up in the morning, think about the many roles that you will be playing that day. As you fill in your log, figure out the role that you have been playing for that activity, but you don' t necessarily have to write it down then and there. This category and the next—End-of-Day Analysis—can be filled in at the end of the day when you find some quiet time for reflection.

END-OF-DAY ANALYSIS

Now for the fun! The very last thing you do each day, just before you turn out the lights, is analyze your log. This is your opportunity to learn something about yourself and, believe it or not, for many people, the results are genuinely surprising. Follow these steps:

1. Begin by totaling the times in the first row. Add up the total for each activity and note it.

2. Review what you've written in the **Activity** column and read across the row to **Role.** Think about what your role has been in each activity and note it in the appropriate place.

3. When you have filled in the entire **Role** column, check back to the **Feelings** column and think about which roles you

found most pleasurable or satisfying. Note as well those activities that you found least pleasurable or satisfying. Give yourself time to think about how you might rearrange your life to maximize your time spent in the pleasurable roles and minimize the time spent in those roles you do not enjoy.

4. Look back at your **Start/Stop/Total** columns and match the total time up against the **Feelings** column. How much time did you spend doing things that offered you very little satisfaction? How much time did you get to spend doing the things you most love to do?

5. Think about what was most surprising in your log and make a note of it. Perhaps it was how much time you spent doing things that you genuinely do not enjoy. Or maybe—hopefully—it was the other way around. Maybe you are surprised by how much pleasure you take in being a manager of people (even an unofficial one). Maybe you are surprised by how little pleasure you get from reporting on a day-to-day basis to somebody else.

6 Repeat this process every day for a week, each day with a new log. At the end of the week, go over all your notes, paying special attention to the **End-of-the-Day Analysis.** Give yourself ample time to think about what you are reading.

Again, the goal here is to reflect. Ultimately, you will want to find enough time in your life to do more of what you love to do and less of what you loathe. In order to achieve that goal, you will need to keep track of the Seven Guiding Principles:

1. Become an active listener.
2. Think outside of the box.
3. Take time to figure out what you find most satisfying.
4. Create time for the things you care about.
5. Learn to enjoy what is in front of you.
6. Learn to be flexible.
7. Prioritize.

Keeping a log and being mindful of the Seven Guiding Principles is only one step toward simplifying your life as a paralegal. The next step involves absorbing the shortcuts and tips you will be hearing from your colleagues in the field. This way, you can learn from others how to make room for the things you most enjoy.

WAR STORIES:
THE PROCRASTINATOR, ESQ.

One of my supervising attorneys was a perpetual and severe procrastinator. Filings would sit on his desk for review for days, weeks, and even months. This caused me much stress and frustration in dealing with case deadlines and client-calling to check on the status of their cases.

My solution was to continually follow up with him on the pending items on his desk, physically putting the documents/filings on his chair or on top of the ever-present pile of items on his desk. Sometimes I'd remind him, or notify him, via e-mail or a phone message or face-to-face of upcoming deadlines and client inquiries on their case status. Sometimes it would get to the point where I'd just have to say to the client that they'd have to take it up with the attorney. The whole business made me pull out my hair sometimes.

CHAPTER 3

Working with Others

What do you call a smiling, courteous person at a bar association convention?

The caterer.

What is the difference between a vulture and a lawyer?

The vulture doesn't get Frequent Flyer miles.

Do you know why a rattlesnake will not bite a lawyer?

Professional courtesy.

These are just three of hundreds, if not thousands, of lawyer jokes that circulate on the Internet. Why is there such an overabundance of these cruel barbs? Because, for some reason, the public antipathy toward the legal profession has escalated exponentially in the last decade. Lawyers are now one of the *least* respected occupations, which is certainly ironic considering that this is a profession that has spawned our nation's Founding Fathers and virtually all of our Presidents, our Supreme Court Justices, and advocates in the fields of labor, women's equality, civil rights, and so forth.

As a paralegal, you not only have to deal with the stigma of being in a field that so many people look at disapprovingly, but you may also feel, to some degree, that this bias has some basis. Although your average lawyer is surely not the money-grubbing, amoral rattlesnake/vulture of these jokes, he or she may embody certain traits that are thought of as being characteristic among practitioners in the field: an intensity that can turn into a ruthless compulsion to win; a relentless and even brutal work ethic; a demanding and exacting way of interacting with others.

Working with attorneys can be enormously stimulating and rewarding, but let it be said that most attorneys are not among the world's most low-key individuals. There *are* certain rigors that feature into being part of a legal team, and those rigors are overlaid on the general difficulties that we all face in the workplace: competition; insensitivity; harassment; and more. This chapter will explore how you, as a paralegal, can deal with difficult individuals and thereby turn your team experience into a winning one.

THE ROLE YOU PLAY

Before we explore the specific dynamics that enter into your being a member of a legal team, it is helpful to look at the fundamental ways in which we all interact with the world. We learn our methods of interacting at a very early age—in fact, these methods begin to kick in at a preverbal stage, when we are infants. It is difficult to remake ourselves, but it is important to look at who we are and to judge what we are doing well and what we could be doing better.

Back in elementary school, you probably received a grade on your report card under the rubric "Works and Plays Well With Others." Were you Excellent, Good, Satisfactory, or Unsatisfactory? Regardless of our grades back then, the truth is that we are all *still* being graded on our skills in this area. Every day of our lives, people are scrutinizing us—our bosses, our managers, our co-workers, our clients—judging whether we are excellent, good, okay, or really not so good at getting along with other people.

Some of us are blessed with sunny personalities and the ability to attract others into our orbits. Such people are often natural leaders who manage to convince others to do things their way; they are sought out and sought after, whether the context is professional or social. Others among us are quiet, reserved, or even shy. Entering a group is always a challenge that we have to "rehearse" for. Our interactions are rarely spontaneous, but they can still be successful and satisfying. Still others among us have significant problems fitting into a group in any constructive way. We may be argumentative, hypercritical, sarcastic, suspicious, quick to pass judgment, ungenerous, even mean-spirited or downright pathological.

Personalities are a complicated issue, but fortunately most of us can learn new and useful ways to interact. In this course of this chapter, you will hear from your fellow paralegals on how they have improved their interrelationships, with specific attention paid to such matters as conflict resolution, dealing with difficult people, mentoring, and more.

COMMUNICATION BASICS

Good relationships begin with good communication. If you can not make your wants and needs known, or, on the flip side, if you can not hear the wants and needs of others, then you are going to have a hard time being part of a team.

❖ *Everything* is communication, not just the words that come out of your mouth. My boss and I have worked together so long that he doesn't have to say a word to let me know how he feels. The arch of his back gives him away. It's all there, in the expression on his face, the way he makes eye contact, his body language . . . all that stuff telegraphs messages to me just as fast, if not faster, than words do. So if you want someone to get a message—or maybe even more important, if you *don't* want them to get a message—then keep your body language in mind.

❖ I've been a paralegal for thirty years and I think one of the biggest changes in the workplace has come from the globalization that is going on in the world. Right now, in our office, we have a person from Cambodia and another from Ecuador. So when you're talking about communication, you've really got to keep in mind cultural differences. For instance, in our culture, if someone is looking down at the ground, you're apt to think that he has something to hide. And yet, in other cultures, looking down can be a sign of deference or respect. Now that's a big difference.

❖ I used to work with a woman who was in many ways a very good person, but she had this one habit that used to drive me insane. She never observed space barriers! When she spoke to me, we were practically nose-to-nose. As far as I'm concerned, there can be no healthy communication when somebody is invading my personal space. I read somewhere that family, lovers, and close friends tend to stand about a foot apart when interacting. Everyone else should observe the four-foot to twelve-foot minimum.

❖ For me, good communication always starts with having a pleasing quality to your voice. If you're shrill or if you swallow your words, that gives people a message about who you are—and maybe, unfortunately, the wrong message. If you suspect that the very sound of your voice may be putting people off, ask a friend to give you a "voice test." Where does your voice need to be softened? Where could it use some strengthening? Do you remember the story of the Greek orator Demosthenes? He learned to speak clearly by putting marbles in his mouth and compensating. We ought to be able to improve the way we speak without having to go to such lengths.

❖ I have to make an admission: I suffer from selective attention. I could be talking to somebody and if I see something else going on out of the corner of my eye, my attention wanders. I used to do this unchecked until somebody once called me on it and said something like, "I'm sorry I'm so uninteresting." I was mortified! So now that I realize I have this problem, I go to special lengths to focus in on the person I'm talking to. I turn my chair around; I look into the person's eyes; I do every conscious thing I can think of to make up for my bad habit.

❖ Learning to listen is a skill like everything else. If you practice your golf swing, chances are you'll get better at it. Same thing with listening: the more you practice, in a conscious way, the better you'll get at it. There are listening skills to learn and listening issues to become aware of. There are techniques, for instance, like reflective listening, where you confirm what you've heard, or think you've heard, by asking questions of the person speaking to you. For instance, if your boss has asked you to file a deposition by the following Tuesday, you might say something like, "Tuesday is our deadline?" If he says yes, you'll know you heard what you think you heard. Of course, you don't want to do this indiscriminately because it could get on somebody's nerves. But, when used selectively, reflective listening might give you some much-needed confidence about your listening skills.

❖ I find reflective listening useful because it initiates dialogue, and good dialogue is worth its weight in gold. For instance, there have been times when my boss will say to me, "I don't know if you are up to this," and I'll say something right back, like, "It seems you're unsure of my capabilities." Basically, I've just restated what he's said (or at least what he's implied) but I'll say it in a very neutral, uncharged way and soon we've got a dialogue going. You have to understand too that a lot of people are basically sort of narcissistic and they love to have their words come back to them in any form. So, in that way, reflective listening also takes on the bonus of being a kind of stroking that you can do at a very small price.

❖ A very important communication technique is called "mirroring." I find myself using it a lot. In the course of an interview with a client, for instance, you "mirror" back to the client things about herself: the way she answers a question with a question, let's say, or the way she holds her head, or crosses her legs. This is a very fast and effective way of building trust and it paves the way toward real exchange.

❖ A big part of communication has to do with asking good questions. Some people never seem to ask questions. Others are full of them. I like the latter. Asking questions shows curiosity and interest and a quality of being present in the moment. In fact, not only do I encourage our support staff to ask questions, but I also teach them how to get into a questioning mode. I advise them to look at any given situation with question words in mind, like Who? What? Where? When? Why? and How?

❖ In our office, we have a policy of communication equality. That means everyone has an equal right to speak. No one, not even the attorneys, are allowed to spout or bloviate at will.

❖ I think an important aspect of communication is putting yourself in the shoes of the person you're communicating with. What do you sound like? Are you prepared to say what you want to say in as brief and cogent a way as possible? (Never forget that in a law office, time is money!). Have you picked a good time to have this exchange? And is there an agenda to what you want to say or are you just wandering all over the place?

❖ Communication is a two-way street. We all know we shouldn't talk too loud or too soft; we shouldn't stick our faces into somebody else's face. But what about the job of the listener? We all need to learn how to become active listeners. That means if somebody's losing you or boring you to tears or speaking too quickly or whatever, you use cues, verbal or otherwise, to let him know it. Saying "Excuse me" or clearing your throat or putting up a hand even . . . whatever you've got to do to get the speaker back on track.

PERSONALITY AND ATTITUDE

As a paralegal, you will be dealing, day-to-day, hour-to-hour, with people: your boss, the other members of your office staff, and clients, as well as the contacts you draw upon in doctor's offices, insurance firms, other legal offices, and so on. In assessing how you deal with people, make a distinction between personality and attitude. One can have an introverted personality and yet have a positive attitude about other people. Conversely, one can be extroverted but still be fundamentally mistrustful or contemptuous of others. Attitude, on the other hand, is influenced by or even formed by our environment—all the things we learn and take away from our parents, teachers, peers, even books and movies. We many not be able to change characteristics that we were born with, but we can change our attitudes.

❖ I come from a long line of victims. My mother, my grandmother—they were abused women. I had to learn a different way of being. The big challenge for me earlier in my career was to learn how to be assertive. I had to get comfortable with standing up for myself, with learning to say no, and with asking for what I wanted. It wasn't easy.

❖ I learned the secret of assertiveness from my sister-in-law, who's a psychologist. She knew I was having trouble navigating the waters in my office and so she taught me this three-step process. The key phrases are "I feel . . . I want . . . I will." If things are not going your way, for instance, you might say to yourself, *I feel* I'm being taken advantage of in this situation. The next piece in the dialogue would be the *"want"* piece: *I want* to be valued as a person. And then you go on to the *will*, which is the determination. "*I will* make it known that I do not allow myself to be treated disrespectfully." It's a pretty powerful construct.

❖ Assertiveness was a major problem for me during my first few years in the field. As time went on, however, I learned how. It's a survival technique. You cannot swim with the sharks if you're a guppy.

❖ There are certain values that are not given their due, the way they were in the past. We live in an era of Jerry Springer and Ricki Lake, where everyone says everything that's on their little minds to the entire world. I personally think there's a lot to be said for some of those more traditional values, like "tact" and "discretion." I'm not even talking about confidentiality, which is obviously a huge issue in our profession. I'm talking about a kind of self-discipline that keeps you from shooting off at the mouth.

❖ Reframing is an important concept to help you adjust your attitude. Reframing essentially allows you to change the meaning of an event. For instance, you might perceive a criticism from your boss as a putdown or even a devastating ego blow. Reframing lets you put the brakes on those feelings. For instance, you might reframe by saying, "Oh, she's just having a bad day" (if, in fact, you think you didn't screw up the way your boss said you did). Later, your boss might very well come to you with an admission that she *was* having a bad day, and your not taking things to heart will have mattered to her.

❖ Don't make an opera or a Shakespearean tragedy out of every little thing. To resist that impulse is something that comes with maturity, but it's never too early to start learning. Let a co-worker's inappropriate comment roll off your back. Before you know it, you'll forget it even happened.

❖ In order to embody the kind of positive attitude that will make you a valuable part of a team, you've got to learn how to receive criticism. Over the years, I've watched people receive criticism in a variety of ways. Some withdraw; others rationalize. Some project, trying to blame others. All of us sometimes do one or the other of these things, and all of these responses are perfectly normal defense mechanisms, but you have to get beyond them in order to find more constructive ways to handle negative feedback.

❖ When I get negative feedback, I have to first ask myself whom it's coming from. Do I respect this person? If not, I pay only so much attention. If the answer is yes, then I listen and I ask for specific information. If I find over the long run that I can't respect the person talking to me, then I know I have to find another job. Believe me, I've been there.

❖ I have this to say about criticism: let it sink in. Don't feel you have to respond to it right away, or at all. Take your time and mull it over.

❖ I always go for the "second opinion." For instance, if a boss says to me, "You're disorganized," I'll canvass my family and friends. "Have you noticed that I've seemed kind of disorganized lately? Just how disorganized would you say I am?" It's a reality test and, even if it hurts, it's important to engage in it.

❖ Giving negative feedback can be as hard as getting it, and as a paralegal we often find ourselves in the position of having to give negative feedback to various support staff members. A rule that I was taught and that I've always tried to live by is to criticize people only on those matters that you think they can change. If someone is clearly not a genius, it does no good to say, "You're not very smart." But things like organization and neatness and a sense of responsibility are qualities that most of us can improve upon to some degree or other.

❖ When giving criticism, I try to make sure to package it as positively and constructively as I can and I always criticize specific behaviors, not personality. In other words, instead of saying, "You're so sloppy," I might say something like, "I would appreciate it if you could be more careful when placing the soiled towels in the container." This is actually a technique that I've learned as a parent, when addressing my children. I would never say to my daughter or son, "You're sloppy! You're stupid! You're bad!" I would talk about the behavior: "There's a mess in the kitchen" or "Because you didn't listen to me, the lamp broke." If you think about using that mode of interrelating in the office, you can see how you could avoid a lot of conflict and bad feelings.

❖ Fortunately I work in an office where the theme is respect. Everyone gets treated with respect and, believe me, that's pretty refreshing after some of the situations that I've worked in. Now that doesn't mean that everyone in our office are best buddies and we all go off to Happy Hour every night. But you don't have to be best friends with someone or even like that person so much to treat him or her with respect. You just have to remember that you're part of a team and, to use a cliché, what's good for all is good for one.

❖ Learn how to become a Switzerland. In other words, think "neutrality." Chances are, down the road, someone is going to try to pull you into a conflict and get you to "pick a side." Resist it. And, whatever you do, resist the impulse to gossip. Like spitting out a car window, gossip usually comes back to hit you in the face. Plus, in our field, where confidentiality is so crucial, idle gossip may get you into a mind-frame where your lips are loose. And we all know what loose lips do.

❖ Always keep your private life private. Some people confuse camaraderie in the workplace with real intimacy. Don't fall into that trap. Save intimacy for your intimate friends and the family members that you trust. Your life can turn miserable in a second if you've told somebody something about yourself or about someone else (particularly another co-worker or a client!) that you shouldn't have.

❖ Be concerned not only with your own success, but also with the success of others. Stay a little later or come in a little earlier to help out a teammate.

❖ Be generous with your knowledge. I once had an aunt who made the world's best devil's food cake, but she would never share the recipe with anyone. When she died, the cake went to the grave with her. Don't be like my aunt. If you know something, share it. This will make you a valued and important member of the team.

THE OFFICE CULTURE

Although we have been discussing issues of teamwork in this chapter that apply across the board, keep in mind that every situation has its specific characteristics and idiosyncrasies.

❖ Every office has its own culture. Call it the office "personality." I've worked in offices that are very formal and heaven forbid you should call your boss by his first name. Now I work in one where heaven forbid I should call my boss "Mr."

❖ The personality of the office is determined by who's running the ship and who's hiring whom. You're not really going to know a whole lot about the office until you get inside of it. When you're being interviewed, it may all sound like hearts-and-flowers. But when you get there, you discover that it's about as sweet and loving as the court of the Borgias.

❖ Every office has its own infrastructure. Usually there's someone who plays the role of the mediator; someone who's the earth mother; someone who's the bad boy, and so on. You won't really be able to pick up on the roles until you've been there a while. It helps, whenever you start a new job, to pick out a co-worker who looks even vaguely simpatico and to go out to lunch with that person, so you can milk her for whatever she's worth about the office dynamics.

❖ It's important, when talking about office culture, to point out that paralegals work in a really diverse range of settings. Someone working side-by-side with an attorney in a sole proprietorship in Cedar Rapids, Iowa is going to have a very different experience from someone working in the Trust & Estates department of a blue-chip Wall Street firm. Your responsibilities will be different; your stress level will be different; and goodness knows your pay will be different!

❖ I started out working in a sole proprietorship and it was a golden opportunity. It gave me the chance to learn about the broad spectrum of legal tasks, because I was a receptionist, a secretary, an administrator, a manager and, oh yes, a paralegal all wrapped up in one. I received and stamped mail; I organized and maintained a filing system; I interviewed clients and witnesses; I kept the books; I did research; I drafted legal documents; I assisted in trial preparation. Eventually, it got to be too much and something saner beckoned, but I don't regret the experience for a minute.

❖ Occasionally problems will develop in offices because not everyone is clear about the status structure. Some offices like to present themselves as being all cheery and laid-back, but don't believe it for a minute. Every office has its power structure and you'd better understand it. To generalize, the attorneys are top dogs, then come the office managers, who are in charge of procedures, then we paralegals (unless you're in a firm big enough to have a legal-assistant manager, to whom the paralegals will report). Below the paralegals are all the support personnel: the secretaries, receptionists, bookkeepers, file clerks, messengers, etc. That's the way it is—the way of the world—with very little variation when you get down to it.

❖ A word of caution: don't try to lord it over the legal secretaries. It's the worst mistake you can make. You know those TV shows where the intern goes in and tries to lord it over the nurses? That's what I was like on my first job. I went into this firm with my paralegal degree in hand, like Little Miss L.A. Law, and I was a bit high-handed with the secretaries. Well, I soon found myself in the Arctic Zone and it took quite a while for things to thaw out.

❖ The way I see it, paralegals are the lieutenants and legal secretaries are the first sergeants. You don't mess with your first sergeants because they are protecting your you-know-what.

❖ Of course you have to respect the secretaries, but they've got to respect you back. That paralegal degree counts for something, and even if you're young or inexperienced, no legal secretary has the right to treat *you* like the secretary. If that happens, go to your administrator for advice.

❖ The fine line between paralegals and legal secretaries, which in theory should not be so fine, often gets blurred, particularly if you're working in a small office. Theoretically, paralegals should not have to be licking envelopes and secretaries should not be the ones doing legal research, but I've seen it go both ways and I've licked plenty of envelopes in my day.

CONFLICT RESOLUTION

Regardless of where you work, you are bound to come into conflict somewhere along the way. The manner in which you handle and resolve conflict will have a lot to do with your ultimate success in a job and in life in general.

❖ There is no reason why you can't learn "techniques" to help you deal with conflict, even something as simple as counting to ten to help you with your impulse control. In the end, however, there are no real shortcuts. The foundation for healthy conflict resolution always begins with you. When you fully understand who you are and what pushes your buttons, then you can begin to understand others and get a grip on situations that upset you.

❖ Keep in mind that healthy and positive conflict resolution is not going to be taking place in an atmosphere of mistrust and insecurity. If you're working in an office with a lot of "top-down" nuttiness, then you have to expect that you'll be dealing with a lot of conflict.

❖ To resolve conflict successfully, it helps to have an understanding of how anger is handled by different individuals. Some of us grew up in homes where it was taboo to be angry, or, worse yet, where you were expected to smile when you were angry. People who grew up in circumstances like that tend to internalize their anger or become so passive that the aggression comes out in lots of highly inappropriate ways. Other people are your "road-rage" variety who go over the top when venting their anger. Most of us are somewhere in-between. You need to identify your own "anger style" and those of your co-workers in order to find the best and quickest route to conflict resolution.

❖ A lot of conflict is best resolved by the classic tactic of turning the other cheek. Usually, people who give you a lot of grief turn out to be very insecure, unhappy people. You don't have to get down to their level. Be the big one . . . even if you are officially below them on the pecking order.

❖ I think the most effective tool I use when I'm in a conflict is to address the other party with his or her name. When I say, "What is the problem, John?" or "What can we do to work this out, Marie?" it shows that I see these individuals as people and it defuses their anger toward me.

❖ My grandfather used to say something that I carry with me to this day. "It is easy to make an enemy; it is harder to keep a friend." I like that saying because it conveys how precious a good relationship is and how difficult it can be to remedy a damaged friendship.

❖ Wolves do this thing when they get into a fight: one of them takes on a submissive stance and shows its jugular to its adversary. This display usually puts an end to the aggression. I've found it useful to adapt that wolf behavior to conflicts that come my way. I will say to the other person, "You know, I really feel I could use your help to figure a way out of this mess." When I do this, the other person rushes to help me and I never feel that I've been taken advantage of.

❖ I laugh. Not necessarily with the person I'm having the problem with, but I find somewhere in my day and life to have a good guffaw. If I'm having a conflict with someone, I'll go out to lunch with my friend Sandy, who is an absolute riot. She does these amazing impersonations of the people we work with. After an hour with Sandy, I'm feeling no pain. It's like nitrous oxide, and when I go back to work and see the person who's been giving me a hard time, it just doesn't seem to matter so much anymore.

❖ Listen, listen, listen. Then listen some more. And encourage others to do the same. Some people who find themselves in a conflict, particularly attorneys, are so anxious to state their case that they don't even hear what the other person has to say. If you come up against such a person—and in this field you're bound to—gently suggest that they listen to you.

❖ Never say or do anything in haste and never, ever, write anything down! I think one of the worst inventions known to mankind is e-mail, in the sense that too many people, when they're angry, will go to their computer and jot off a furious note. Well, that e-mail becomes an historical record of your anger that you would rather not see again when you're feeling better. Use self-control in all your dealings and don't shoot off (or write off) at the mouth!

❖ Go for a walk. Breathe deeply. Eat a doughnut. Do something to break the chain of the anger. Then you can go back and look at the situation differently and decide what to do next.

❖ I think the key to conflict resolution is a commitment to resolving the conflict. You and the other person have to be on the same page. Make it a page that says, "We *will* get beyond this. We *must* get beyond this."

❖ In order to resolve the conflict, it's important to ask yourself what you're looking for. For some people, it's an apology. The apology is like the pot of gold at the end of the rainbow. I tell people not to be so focused on apologies. Focus on co-existence instead.

❖ When you're trying to iron out a conflict with someone, always stay in the present. *Always.* Never bring up a whole history of slights and insensitivities. Once you start doing that, things will spiral out of control.

❖ Conflict resolution brings into play, once again, the issue of assertiveness. Unfortunately, since the paralegal profession is predominantly female, the age-old gender generalizations are at work. A male paralegal is often seen as assertive, yet a female paralegal in the exact same situation is instead seen as shrill, emotional, or, worse yet, "hormonal." I have found e-mail to be a godsend. I know that some people say not to write stuff down, because it will come back to haunt you, but I disagree. Instead of hallway conversations, you can now retain a written history of the situation, and you can have the benefit of time to more carefully choose your words before responding to someone. I also make a point of gathering as many facts as I can. The more hard facts you have in your corner, the more convincing your point of view will be judged.

DEALING WITH DIFFICULT SITUATIONS

Even if you love your job, there may be aspects of it that you find not to your liking or even quite upsetting. Let us see what your colleagues have to say on this matter.

❖ As a paralegal, my role can encompass a lot of different areas. For example, when the secretarial staff is short-handed, we may be asked to answer the phones or type our own letters or whatever. I don't feel that's a problem because it's always a value, as far as I'm concerned anyway, to foster a team environment. Besides, the converse of that is when my attorney will ask me to analyze a file for a client status report, a job that is typically an attorney responsibility. I look at that as a challenge and I feel lucky that I am working for an attorney who is using me in a substantive role. I would be angry, however, if I was working in a firm where I was asked to get food or run other personal errands. I would go to my paralegal supervisor and discuss it with him or her, or else I'd discuss it in the context of a paralegal meeting.

❖ If I'm asked to take on a task that I don't wish to do, I use the "prioritization" method. Usually, the things I don't like to do are of an administrative-non-billable nature. So I inform the requesting attorney of my workload and that fact that I won't be able to attend to their task for some time (the implication being that I'm doing things I can bill for). I am of the belief that, as a paralegal, I'm here to assist the attorney and to get the project done, but it is the nature of my seniority and high billable rate that has made me more particular about the tasks I take on.

❖ One of the most difficult situations I think that a paralegal is bound to face is when he or she screws up. And, believe me, everyone does screw up. The best policy—in fact, in my mind, the *only* policy—is to come clean. Own up to the mistake. A paralegal should promptly inform an attorney of any serious mistakes, for it might still be possible to rectify the error. If not, at least the attorney will know about it and hopefully not get caught with his pants down, particularly in court, which, if it happens, will be everyone's worst-case scenario.

❖ You've got to own up to your mistakes or otherwise the firm might be looking at a malpractice suit. Since mistakes are an inevitable part of this business, we have the institution of professional courtesy. If you miss a minor deadline, the opposing attorney will most likely extend the courtesy and forgive the mishap, knowing that the same thing could happen the other way around.

❖ Not admitting to mistakes is, at its base, an ethical issue. As a paralegal, if you make a significant error that affects the interests of a client, your attorney's fiduciary duty of loyalty to that client has been breached. By the same token, even though the paralegal doesn't have a direct fiduciary duty to the client, he or she does have such a fiduciary duty to the attorney who is the employer. Breaching that duty is a pretty clear avenue to dismissal.

❖ In my experience, paralegals are frequently asked to do things that are above and beyond their job duties. The most uncomfortable thing I have had to do on a regular basis is to falsify authorizations for release of records due to the fact that someone prior to myself had dropped the ball and had not gotten the necessary medical and/or employment records on a case we were defending. These records are crucial to the case and must be had at almost any cost. It was common practice in my firm for paralegals to falsify these authorizations and "white-out" the old date to insert a new date and copy the form. I went to my boss the first few times it was suggested I do this. He gave me the green light but was careful to add that he didn't want to "know" about it.

❖ My most difficult times in the field were when I was asked to do unethical billing. My job was to inventory the estate of the decedent. I was asked to bill out excessive time, based on the size of the estate, and was very uncomfortable with that. The attorney informed me that this was the basis for my remuneration and he was only looking out for my best interest. Thanks to my training, I knew the practice was unethical and when I continued to chafe at it, the attorney referred me to the office manager, who also tried, though unsuccessfully, to convince me to bill out unethically. Although I continued to do my work and to bill out the correct amount, I had to decide whether this was a place that I wanted to continue to work at and I decided against it. The place had a big turnover anyway, due to these unsound practices, so I knew I wasn't looking at a lot of longevity. I gave notice and fortunately it all turned out well for me, as I got a better job right away.

❖ There are times when you'll find yourself up against the wall, professionally speaking, and it's important to remember that you must never sacrifice your professionalism. Remember at all times the Paralegal Code of Ethics, which compels you to maintain reasonable and accurate billing records. Don't forget that companies and offices can be audited, and if your billing rate or hours are excessive, you could be in serious hot water.

❖ Sure, you're going to be asked to do things you don't want to do—that's the nature of the beast. For me, it was being back-up to the runners. We never seemed to have enough runners and when they were out sick or on holiday or whatever, I was always the one who had to take over. Several months ago, I was asked to go on another run to the courthouse, and I said I would do it, but I wanted to know when other paralegals and secretaries in the firm, who were younger than me and who also knew where the courthouse was, were going to be trained. I said I was closing in on 50 years old and didn't feel I had to be the sole back-up for our twenty-something runners. I have rarely been asked to do runs again. I guess it all boils down to what you won't eat in the end, and when you put your foot down, usually people, if they value you at all, will hear you.

❖ What's helped me as far as the issue of assertiveness goes is taking on more of a leadership role in paralegal organizations. For two years now, I've served as president of our state paralegal association and going around to talk to other paralegals has really boosted my confidence.

❖ There are any number of ways you can deal with difficult situations, and chances are your firm has some policy in place for review of such situations. But there are certain instances, like sexual harassment, which you really should not attempt to deal with off-the-cuff. In the case of sexual harassment or any kind of racial, gender, age, or sex choice bias, discuss the situation with a human resources representative and follow your company's formal measures for dealing with such issues.

❖ There are difficult situations and then there are just plain difficult people. There are no shortage of those in this world, and a lot of them, I hate to say, find their way into law. You know what I do with difficult people? I compliment them—relentlessly. Our office manager, for instance, is a real piece of work. She's staggeringly competent, but the last time anyone saw a smile on her face was in 1991. But I flatter her every inch of the way. "Don't you look nice today, Janis." "That's a great color on you, Janis." "You always know the best restaurants, Janis." Now this may sound nauseating, but it's no skin off my back and it keeps her out of my hair.

❖ One of my girlfriends, also a paralegal, was telling me about this huge blowout she had with a computer support person in her office. This person, whom I'll call Lois, is a terrible troublemaker, a real spoiler kind of personality. My friend was fuming—she was going to tell Lois off; she was going to go to the boss, yadda yadda— and I said, "Hold it right there. Send the cow flowers instead." "What?!" my friend cried. "You heard me," I said. Well, after we went back and forth for a while, my friend did as I suggested and it worked like a charm. At first, my friend thought that to send flowers would be an admission of guilt, but I told her that the more important thing was for her to look like a peacemaker in everyone else's eyes. Which is exactly what happened.

❖ When it comes to dealing with difficult people, simply staying out of their line of vision is the best strategy. It might sound really simplistic, but if you regard avoidance as a real technique, you'll see how effective it is. In my office we have one person who makes Ross Perot look like a cupcake, and when I see him I just duck behind a door.

❖ I think a little sympathy and patience goes a long way toward dealing with difficult people. Some of my friends call me "The Saint" because they know I have this attitude, but I'm comfortable with it. I feel that difficult people often have difficult lives or have had difficult childhoods and I try to forgive them as much as I can.

MENTORING

Mentors are the people who embody qualities, professional and personal, that deserve to be emulated. Being lucky enough to have a mentor—or to be one—can make a world of difference in your professional life. Here are five top tips to keep in mind regarding the mentoring relationship.

- The mentoring relationship is equally valuable for both parties. It's a way for the mentor to give back. In the past, you might have been mentored. Now it's your turn.
- Mentoring is really a two-way street. It's not just about the mentor teaching the mentee. I've learned a lot from my mentees.
- Mentoring people has helped keep me fresh. I continuously brush up my knowledge base by mentoring.
- Neither mentors nor mentees should expect to come away from the relationship with a fast friendship. If it happens, it happens, but that's not the reason for the relationship. The relationship is there for a purpose—a learning purpose—and that's what you need to understand.
- Like anyone in a teaching capacity, mentors should teach to a large extent by using positive reinforcement. Harsh criticism has no place in the mentoring relationship and can quickly end one.

War Stories:
There's a Phone Call for You . . .

My supervising attorney had a severe problem with returning client calls. Most calls were simply ignored and/or never returned. This caused me much stress and frustration since clients would call me for an explanation as well as to complain. Moreover, the clients would start asking me for the answers/information as well as for legal advice that put me in a really precarious position in terms of unauthorized practice of law (UPL).

I dealt with this situation by triaging the numerous piles of messages on a daily basis. I sorted them into those messages that could be handled by the paralegals, those messages that needed immediate response by the attorney, and those that needed the attorney's specific response but were of a lesser priority and could be put back to a later date. For my cases, I assumed a customer service role in handling the clients' complaints as best I could. Whenever and wherever I could, I'd obtain the necessary information from the attorney and would relay her instructions and advice to the client. Any calls regarding complex legal inquiries or serious complaints were automatically referred to the attorney for her to handle.

CHAPTER 4

Stress: The Reality and the Relief

As we pointed out earlier, a certain amount of stress is to be expected when you work as a paralegal. People constantly make demands on you; you have deadlines to meet and scheduling to stay on top of; serious and potentially costly mistakes are always a risk. All of this takes its toll, but, as a professional, you are expected to handle yourself with unimpeachable aplomb, remaining coolly unruffled at all times.

Ridiculous! you say. We're only human!

True, but working in a law firm setting does require you to subscribe to a certain standard of conduct. That means no screaming, no cursing, no throwing of objects, and no more than a faint sheen of perspiration on your upper lip. So how do you manage this? How do you keep cool when the heat is on? This chapter is filled with hints from your colleagues in the field, all on the subject of stress—how to recognize it, how to handle it, and how to beat it.

THE STRESS FACTOR

One reason why stress enters into the work of the paralegal is because law, like medicine, touches on a lot of elemental nerves in people's lives. As a paralegal, you may be dealing with wills, bankruptcies, accident claims, marital problems, and custody arrangements, not to mention all the corporate and governmental issues that have huge amounts of money riding on them, and for many paralegals, you have to worry about your billable hours on top of it all. There are also deadlines to meet and combative personalities to deal with (often within your own office!). In other words, stress comes with the territory.

❖ There is a ton of stress in this type of job. If you are not a very organized person, there is chronic stress. In fact, even if you are a very organized person, stress is a problem. The deadlines around trials and all make the stress intermittent in nature, which I find the worst. No matter how organized you try to be, your attorney will almost always have a slew of last-minute details that he needs help with. Trial exhibits, for example, stress me out totally.

❖ There is a lot of stress in my job in that the pace of the practice I'm involved in is not constant. If I woke up in the morning knowing what the day would be like, it would be helpful. But for me the stress ebbs and flows, which makes it difficult to plan for the stress and to get myself fortified.

❖ Stress in my job is intermittent and mostly dependent upon deadlines, competing priorities or the number of priority or expedite cases, client interaction, and the demands and volume of the caseload. These factors change instantaneously and unexpectedly and can, in the blink of an eye, change my day from a low-stress one to a high-stress one.

❖ I experience tons of stress. Litigation is famous for it. It is chronic, with intermittent spikes, such as during trial prep.

❖ The stress in my current job, which is in the corporate sector, is generally intermittent and mostly manageable. I have worked in other law firms that do litigation where the stress was much higher and the environment was more often stressful than not stressful. When I realized how much I was popping antacids, I decided it was time for a change.

❖ One area of stress for me has been around the issue of billable hours. I needed to be in the office on Saturdays, at least for a few hours, to keep the billable hours up. Then I discovered that if I just kept working during the week and didn't waste time doing personal things or working on the tasks for the paralegal association I'm involved with, I could easily get my billable hours in between 9 and 5 and have Saturday back for myself. That's helped a lot.

❖ My best advice is to learn that the desk will never—*not ever*—be clear. Once you realize that, things get a little easier.

STRESS: A SOCIETAL PROBLEM

We live in a stressful world. Many of us are seriously sleep-deprived. We don't get nearly enough vacation time in this country compared to European nations, where workers typically receive two whole months of paid vacation a year. Issues like childcare become a source of major stress for many American employees, with the stress factor going through the roof when children get sick and can't go to their regular childcare providers. Baby boomers are particularly stressed as "the sandwich generation," taking care of young children and aged parents at the same time. Furthermore, many of us commute along traffic-clogged thoroughfares to jobs that are often shaky due to the consolidation that is happening all over the economic landscape. Take all of that and throw into the mix the emotional aftermath of 9/11, and we have a very stressed population indeed. And all of this does not take into account the major stressors that occur in people's personal lives: deaths, divorces, economic reversals, and so on.

❖ You know those charts that show stress points correlating to life events? Well, this year I went through the roof. My husband and I separated. My mother was no longer able to live on her own and I had to get her into a life care facility. I developed phlebitis. To tell you the truth, I didn't know what end was up and I had to find some way of dealing with it all. I tried a lot of things like meditation and exercise and all that, but in the end I really needed to get on an anti-anxiety drug. It's made all the difference.

❖ Sometimes you don't even know how stressed you are until you start acting peculiarly and people call you on it. "Why are you eating so fast?" "Why are you walking so fast?" "Why are you sleeping in the middle of the day?" "Look at your mouth—you're grimacing." These are telltale signs of stress.

❖ The way I manifest stress is through fatigue. I become utterly exhausted. I go home; I eat a frozen dinner; I get into bed with a hot water bottle . . . in July! No, seriously—I become completely and dangerously depleted. It's scary.

❖ When I'm stressed out, I do this thing where I tell myself I'm feeling fine, but the fact is I'm not fine. At such times, I get very compulsive about doing things that I hope will make me feel better. Things like eating chocolate. My chocolate consumption will spike off the charts. Or I'll suddenly start spending money. I'll go out

---

RECOGNIZING SIGNS OF STRESS

Stress impacts us in any number of ways. See if you answer to any of the following:

Physical   Digestive problems, headache, neck pain, skin rashes, muscle tension, elevated blood pressure, flare-ups of illnesses like arthritis or asthma

Thought processes   Memory issues, impatience, procrastination, obsessive behavior

Emotional   Depression, irritability, helplessness, anxiety, anger, bitterness, conflicts with co-workers

---

and buy four pairs of shoes in one fell swoop. I suppose it could be worse. I had a girlfriend who, when she was under stress, would become completely promiscuous. Instead of buying four pairs of shoes, she'd sleep with four different guys in the course of four days! But the compulsion comes from the same place: the attempt to make yourself feel good internally by doing something externally. The problem is it never works.

❖ There's stress and then there's stress. It's not so terrible to have some stress in your life. I even find that stress can be energizing to some degree. Of course, some people can't handle any of it—I had a cousin who gave up her accounting practice (too much stress at tax time) and moved up to Vermont to start a handmade quilt business. But don't fool yourself—there's stress in the quilt business too. Stress is just a part of life.

❖ We hear so much about stress in the media these days that people feel if they have any of it, they're going to keel over. Things like tight deadlines, fights with your husband or kids or mother or father, or money problems are perfectly normal. You need to learn how to suck it up and not make a federal case out of everything.

❖ Some stress is acceptable and inevitable, but "some stress" is not the same as constant, intense stress. I know what that's like, having worked for a certifiable lunatic for 16 months. Constant stress means that you're in a perpetual state of "fight or flight." Your body's trying to figure out its next move. That means more adrenaline release, increased heart flow and blood pressure, more sugar from the liver . . . all unhealthy stuff. Over time, that constant stress can result in ulcers, migraines, hypertension, asthma, and there are even links to cancer and cardiovascular disease. Constant stress also suppresses the immune system, which means you're more likely to come down with colds, flu, or worse. Remember: you only get one go-round in this lifetime, so don't squander it on stressful environments.

❖ To my way of thinking, there's a difference between "stress" and "distress." Stress is what you cope with on a day-to-day basis, along with the rest of the human race. It's traffic and your mother-in-law and noise and waiting in line at the bank and so on. Distress is what you get when the stress is prolonged and feels inescapable. That's when your body starts reacting with migraines and ulcers and colitis and all those other ills that can become so serious over time.

Coming at You from All Four Corners

Stress is at its worst when it seems completely surrounding and inescapable. When that happens, you have to look at your part in the situation. How are you making stress worse? What are you doing wrong?

❖ As far as I'm concerned, stress is incredibly exacerbated by negativity. For instance, everyone knows that right before a trial you're going to encounter a ratcheting-up of the stress quotient. That's just the way it goes. And I can deal with that. What I can't deal with is this other paralegal in my office who starts saying things like, "We're never going to get this done! We're sunk! We might as well throw in the towel!" I just want to haul off and punch her. But, since that would not be appropriate behavior in a law office, I try to stay outside of her negative orbit as much as I can. Sometimes, however, I have to admit that the centrifugal force of her negativity sucks me in.

❖ I've had to learn to be more flexible. I'm now ready to admit that I was a bit of a control freak. "Queen of Mean," my boyfriend used to call me. It's just that I had very high expectations and when they didn't get met, I was not a happy camper. But now I understand that this is not a good way to live. If you hear yourself saying "should" and "ought" and "must" all the time, then something's wrong.

❖ Get real. That means you have to develop an understanding of what you can and cannot do. Unrealistic expectations and demands will compromise your attitude about life enormously. You are not Superwoman. You cannot do it all.

❖ You need to learn to say the "N" word: "No." No no no no no. See? It's not so hard. "No. It's my son's graduation tomorrow." "No, I have a medical appointment I cannot reschedule." "No. That is not a task I feel I should be asked to do, as I've already explained to you." Think of "No" as a beautiful word—the jewel in your crown.

❖ Watch what comes out of your mouth. Hostile and aggressive talk—what the kids call "trash talk"—is only going to make a stressful situation that much worse, like throwing fat on the fire. And once you say something, you can't un-say it.

❖ I cannot bear it when people say, "I'm only trying to give you constructive criticism." That's usually such a phony smokescreen for, "I'm only trying to dump all over you." I think a great rule to keep in mind, to have sewn onto a sampler or crocheted onto a pillow or whatever, is "The only person you can really change is yourself." It's so true. Too many of us have tried to change our spouses or our children or our parents or our bosses or our friends or co-workers, and how many of us have done so with any kind of success? I sure don't know any. Devote your energies instead to thinking about how you can change yourself, not what you can change in other people.

❖ Acceptance is a word that is out of favor these days. All we hear about instead is "empowerment." Well, I'm all for empowerment, but sometimes the gentler charms of acceptance can be very healing too. You can look at a situation and say, "I'm not going to be able to do anything about this but I'm not ready to leave. So can I accept what's here and make the best of it?" Sometimes the answer is no, and you move on. Other times, in just asking the question, you come upon answers.

❖ There's no question that a lot of stress is brewed in the pressure cooker of your office, but so many times it's more related to what's going on outside of the office. If you're having problems with your partner, for instance, or with your kids or parents or a friend, you're going to have stress in your life, and meeting the demands of a stressful job just becomes that much harder. You can also have stress from factors that have nothing to do with your interrelationships with other people. For instance, you might be having a bad reaction to some allergen in the air that is causing your body stress. When you are physically in stress, the emotional stress just goes along for the ride.

❖ There are people in my office who deal with stress by taking anti-anxiety drugs and that's fine, as long as you're carefully following doctor's orders. Some of my co-workers, however, deal with stress by getting bombed after work or by stepping outside every hour for a smoke and, as far as I'm concerned, that's not fine. To me, the way to deal with stress is by finding even a small amount of time every day to go inside of yourself and to connect with your spiritual side. Whether you do that by meditation, prayer, yoga, a walk in the woods or in the park, or simply by deep breathing is up to you. But you've got to do it.

STRESS RELIEF

Ultimately, there are certain situations that prove themselves untenable, in terms of the amount of stress they deliver. For instance, if you work for an attorney who you know is a crook and if you expect the FBI to walk through the door at any moment with an indictment for you in the bargain, there is no way you are going to get around stress and your best option may be to simply run the other way. But, for those who are in more mainstream situations that have "normal" levels of stress, there are any number of stress-relief techniques you can draw upon.

Let's All Take a Deep Breath Now

❖ Deep breathing always helps me relax. The trick is to inhale deeply through your nose, filling your lungs. Hold the breath until you count to six. Then don't just let it all out, but exhale it slowly, once again counting to six. If you do this for several minutes, you'll be amazed by the results.

❖ I do this Zen-type thing when I'm deep breathing. I say (mostly to myself), "In with the good" on the inhalations and "Out with the bad" on the exhalations. It's a simple way to persuade my mind that it's ridding itself of toxins.

❖ Some people are so stressed out that when they try deep breathing that they're afraid they're going to hyperventilate. Hyperventilation is awful and it's not an uncommon manifestation of stress, but deep breathing doesn't lead to it. If, however, you find yourself getting lightheaded, you should, of course, stop immediately.

Communication Helps

❖ A good deal of stress can be ameliorated by the constructive expression of your feelings. I was walking around like a time bomb, completely bottled up, until my next-door neighbor called me on it. He said, "Is something the matter, Pat? You don't seem yourself." When he said that, it was, like, whoa! I wasn't myself. In fact, I didn't know who I was. So I began talking more—to him, to other friends and neighbors, to my family. When people said, "How are you?" I didn't answer "Fine" like an automaton. I told them how I really was . . . whether they liked it or not.

❖ I haven't got much community where I live. I'm single and I only moved to Chicago a year ago, for work. I was lonely and hadn't anybody to talk to about the kind of stress I was going through. But I wandered into a chat room on the Internet and it was just what the doctor ordered. I know you have to be careful about such places, but I've made some great cyber-friends on this site, and when I feel the anxiety getting to me at two or three in the morning, I can always log in and find somebody to unload on.

❖ Stress drove me back to the church. I swore I'd never go back, because it just hadn't worked for me in the past, but this time I joined a congregation that had this great pastor, really forward-thinking and intellectually alive, and he's been an enormous help to me as far as finding ways to deal with my stress at work.

❖ I had constant, unyielding stress at work and I couldn't quit. I wasn't sure it would be that easy for me to find another job in my chosen field, and I'd just gone through a divorce and needed a regular paycheck. In other words, I felt stuck. So stuck that I developed this awful case of acid-reflux. Every night, I felt like I was having a heart attack, which, as you can imagine, did not exactly help my overall stress quotient. I wound up going to a counselor, a marvelous social worker who helped me get a handle on some of my stress. I don't know why I had to wait until it got so bad to help myself that way.

❖ I've got a parakeet. Name of Lucy. I'm not nuts—believe me. I used to have a dog, but the stress of having to run home and walk him was just more stress that I didn't need. Then I had a cat but I was violently allergic to her. So I wound up with a bird, which I was very dubious about, but she's been the best pet! There's not a lot I have to do for her, and she likes to be talked to. Every night I tell her about my idiot boss—let's call him Mr. Nameless—and now she squawks, "Uh-oh! Here comes Mr. Nameless!" It's great for a laugh.

Being Good to Your Body

❖ There is absolutely no stress-reliever that compares to regular vigorous exercise. Believe me, I've been on anti-anxiety drugs and I've exercised and, as I say, there's no comparison. Walking, running, swimming, biking, jazz dancing . . . whatever works for you. Just keep at it and learn to love it, because you will. Once you feel those endorphins being released in your system, you'll come to fully appreciate the curative powers of exercise.

❖ Exercise doesn't have to be exercise that you don't enjoy in order for it to be good for you. In fact, it should never be exercise you don't enjoy! Tennis, soccer, inline skating, aerobic dancing . . . they're all great. Just make sure it's regular.

❖ Do something physical every day, even if it's just walking for 15 minutes. You've got to keep up your endurance if you're going to work with attorneys, because they can be challenging as well as draining!

❖ I indulge myself in a massage every now and then. It's the nicest thing I do for myself. Just knowing that I can do something for myself that feels that good gives me a kind of strength to get through the hard stuff.

❖ A hot tub, every night, is my prescription. I splurge on fabulous bath waters that smell divine. After all, you only live once.

❖ My cure for stress is sleep. I know a lot of people can't sleep when they're stressed, but for me it's the opposite. I make a point of getting into bed before 10 p.m. with some Celtic music on and a lavender candle burning and I'm good for eight hours.

❖ If you're under a lot of stress (and who isn't these days?), make sure you get your B vitamins. Calcium too. Stay away from foods that put a lot of stress on your body, like colas, fried foods, chips, junk food, white sugar, all that stuff. Eating a lot of raw foods is also beneficial in a stress situation.

❖ I got better at coping with stress once I weaned myself from caffeine. It's a personal decision, but, if you're suffering from stress, you might want to experiment with substituting a nice herbal tea for some of that coffee or Earl Grey you've been chugging. Some herbs, which you'll find in teas, have natural stress-relieving properties. Chamomile, rose hips, ginseng . . . check it out.

❖ Water, water everywhere! That's the key. Our bodies are 60 to 70 percent water, so you have to replenish whatever you lose. The more you hydrate, the better you'll feel and function. I try to drink at least eight eight-ounce glasses a day. (Don't overdo, however, and drink gallons. That can cause problems too).

❖ I always take a large container of spring water to work with me and keep it close by. And I always drink before I get thirsty. When you fall behind and are trying to play a catch-up game with hydration, it's twice as hard to get it right.

❖ Some people feel that anything liquid that goes into their bodies is hydrating. Baloney! Keep in mind too that certain substances, like the caffeine in tea and coffee, can act as diuretics, causing water to leave your body. So don't depend on those beverages to hydrate you.

❖ I always pay attention to my diet to make sure that I've got a lot of variety. That way, I figure I'm covering my bases. If I eat dairy, grains, fruits, veggies, a little chicken or fish, then I can feel pretty confident that I'm getting what I need. This means that I never go on diets where

I'm mostly eating grapefruits or cabbage soup or steak or what have you.

❖ You want to hear a revolutionary concept? Don't eat when you're not hungry. Most of the time you're doing that, you're just trying to alleviate stress, which can be better dealt with by a few minutes of deep breathing or maybe a walk outside. You'd be amazed how much easier it is to keep your weight under control when you pay attention to your stomach hunger instead of your mouth hunger.

❖ My mother used to tell me to chew each bite of food fifty times. I couldn't stand it when she said that, but now I realize that there is a lot of sense to it. As an adult, I find that if I eat slowly and chew my food thoroughly, I eat a lot less and I have a lot less stomach distress.

❖ You want to know my secret to eating healthy? Make a nice meal out of every meal you have. For breakfast I always make sure there's some beautiful fruit on the plate. For lunch I often have a thermos of hot soup and a wrap. For dinner, even if I'm by myself, I put down a placemat, I pour myself a glass of wine, and I eat a leisurely and relaxing meal. I think grabbing your food and gulping it down on the run is the worst thing you can do for yourself, and making a nice ritual out of every meal is an incredibly effective stress-reliever as well.

Laughter and Other Therapies

❖ To me, the best thing you can do is laugh. Laughter is like flushing your system of stress. It's such a powerful weapon.

❖ I once read somewhere how women don't like The Three Stooges. Well then, I must be an exception to the case. After a harrowing day at work, I like nothing more than to get home, put on my p.j.'s, turn on the phone machine, cook up a big plate of spaghetti, and sit down in front of the VCR with a Stooges tape. When Moe pokes Larry and Curly in the eyes, all my troubles evaporate, at least for the moment.

❖ I urge everyone to check out Loretta LaRoche. She writes about laughter as therapy, and you can get her audiotapes to listen to in the car. When she's on, I don't even mind sitting in bumper-to-bumper traffic. Check out her website at www.stressed.com.

❖ Yoga is my savior. I discovered it a few years ago, when my daughter made me take a class with her. Now I don't know how I ever lived without it. In addition to making my body feel like a better place for me to inhabit, yoga creates a timespace that is so different than what I'm usually in that when I'm doing it, it feels almost like a little vacation.

❖ I keep a journal. It helps me get a handle on my stress to know that I have a place to put down my feelings of gloom and anxiety. Somehow the journal acts to contain them.

❖ My best stress reducer is a cassette tape that my three nieces made when they were little, singing children's songs. The sound of them singing "The Farmer in the Dell" is like medicine to me. Everybody else in my office thinks I'm crazy, but I do make a point of listening to it with headphones!

❖ I've got a secret weapon against stress: vacations! Seriously, a lot of us forget to take them, particularly if you're working for yourself, as freelance paralegals like myself do. The therapeutic effect of a vacation can be enormous. Even a day off, when you're feeling really stressed out, can make a world of difference. Spend the day bicycling or pack a picnic and head for the beach. You'll feel like a new person.

❖ For me, it's hobbies. My friends think I'm crazy, but I like to build birdhouses. I've made about 400 of them so far. I'm running out of people to give them to.

❖ Introduce as much beauty into your life on a daily basis as you can. Maybe that means buying fresh flowers or listening to Mozart on a Walkman to and from work or just noticing the sunsets. Whatever it is, beauty heals.

BODY WOES

Problems in your physical presentation—the way you stand, sit, walk, and so on—can also impact enormously on your stress quotient. Unhealthy or defective body postures can cause a number of musculoskeletal problems, particularly when these postures become habit. Here are some ideas from your colleagues about how to keep your body healthy and functioning at peak level in the workplace.

❖ When I started on my first job, this terrific woman took me under her wing and became a real mentor to me. One of the first things she did was to give me a mini-course on overall posture. It has kept me in good shape all the years since. Basically, she gave me a set of rules that I have always followed and it goes like this: Head up and chin level with the floor; neck elongated and balanced directly above the shoulders; chest out and up; shoulders level, spine straight; abdomen flat; hips level horizontally; knees slightly flexed and positioned over the feet. This is something you've got to learn how to do, and learning it is not so easy, but once you've got it down, it will protect you for your whole career.

❖ The most physically exhausting thing is to sit for long stretches at the computer. I try to do ankle and foot exercises while I'm working and then stand, stretch, and walk around the building every couple of hours.

❖ Just as important as your standing posture is your sitting posture. The one thing I always tell the people who do the kind of work we do is slide your rear to the rear. It takes discipline to do that. Many of us sprawl in our chairs. But, if you tuck your tush into the back of the chair, your body will be grateful.

❖ When you're sitting, keep your back straight and the soles of your feet on the floor. Don't cross your legs or your feet at the ankle. Your soles on the floor give you support.

❖ You know what makes me laugh? And then makes me shake my head with pity? High heels! High heels are one step up the evolutionary food chain from foot-binding. There is no way a woman can wear high heels and not encounter musculoskeletal problems down the line. Whether the heels are chunky or narrow doesn't matter—both sorts apply pressure to the knees, which you need like . . . well, like pressure to the knees. They also throw off your center of gravity, and leave you open to a host of problems like back pain and arthritis. And, I hate to say it, but in this age of terrorism, if you have to run fast, how are you going to do it in heels?

❖ Get yourself a good pair of shoes. No, get yourself at least two good pairs of shoes. Something nice and wide and low-heeled that will absorb shock and give your toes the room they need. Don't leave home without them!

❖ If your office is not carpeted, treat yourself to a cushioned mat for your work area. It'll go a long way toward beating fatigue.

❖ All of us working in this field are very susceptible to CTDs. That's cumulative trauma disorders, in case you didn't know. We sit a lot and hold our bodies in unnatural positions for long periods of time, which means we're contracting our muscles. This can lead to problems of the hand, wrist, shoulders, neck, back, feet, and legs. Prevention is the key here. You've got to fit your work to your body, not your body to your work.

❖ If you work in an environment that has any physical discomfort built into it, as most of us do, try to counter the problem by including regular stretching intervals in your schedule to break up the repetitiveness of the motions you use.

❖ Eye soreness and burning of the eyes from staring at a computer most of the day is a big problem. I take breaks away from the computer regularly and I wear my glasses a few days each week (not every day, because total dependence on glasses just weakens the eyes). Stretching out my neck from side to side also helps.

❖ I try to organize my workload so that I'm not just doing one thing for a long, uninterrupted amount of time. If I cannot get around that, then I take mini-breaks, maybe one or two minutes every half hour. I will stretch, close my eyes, walk to the bathroom (the most acceptable place to go), or get some water.

❖ Get your eyes examined regularly. Most paralegals work on computers doing research for long periods of time and that takes a toll. I had to get reading glasses that I wear with my contacts to alleviate my headaches.

❖ It can be very fatiguing to dictate. You are expending much oxygen when you dictate and are in a sitting position. You need to learn to walk away for a while and then come back to it later.

❖ Document reviews, where you are faced with moving around hundreds of boxes, can be exhausting. Also, the last week before and the week of trial are typically very long days with little time for routine exercise and so forth. It's important to keep limber, by stretching, and taking short breaks, maybe even just for a breath of air, during such circumstances.

❖ I've found that exercising during lunch a few times a week helps me to handle the body aches and pains associated with or derived from sitting or stooping over a desk and computer all day.

❖ Just carrying a loaded briefcase to work every day starts you off with a posture deficit. You're imbalanced by that weight and you need to find movements that compensate for that stress on your body. For me, Pilates has been the answer.

❖ I've learned a rule from my chiropractor: start the day off with the "hug your best friend" routine. You wrap your arms around your body and you turn as far as you can to the left, then as far as you can to the right. Wait till you see how good that feels!

❖ Abdominal crunches are your insurance against serious back pain and weakness. You don't have to pack a six-pack, but you do need to give the abs some attention.

❖ You want to know what was really killing me? Putting a heavy tote over one shoulder, filled with all my work, my novel of the moment, my organizer, and who only knows what else, and going off to the office. I really did a number on myself that way. Now I use a backpack. Okay, so maybe I look a little bit like something other than the 52-year-old woman I am, but I don't care. It helps the body of this 52-year-old woman immeasurably. I was told, however, that you mustn't overload your backpack. A loaded backpack should not exceed 15% of your weight, and should never weigh more than 25 pounds.

❖ I got totally into using a backpack too. What's a perfect backpack? Lightweight material to start out with (not leather!). Adjustable, wide, padded shoulder straps and a waist strap too. The heavier items you put closer to the back, and it's good to have a pack that has a lot of pockets, so you can play around with distributing the weight.

❖ Here's a cardinal rule: always sit with your back against the back of the chair. That's so important. Your knees should be level with your hips. You might want to get a footrest to achieve this. I also like to put a pillow at the small of my back for support, or you could use a rolled-up towel for that purpose.

❖ Keep those shoulders straight, paralegals! Don't slouch or lean forward to look at your work or your monitor.

❖ Here's your keyboard etiquette: keyboard and mouse should be kept close to the edge of the desk and they should be positioned so that your arms fall naturally to your sides. Support your wrists with a gel pad or a wrist support.

❖ Have you analyzed your typing style? Some people are "heavy" typers and they're bound for trouble. Heavy typing, over time, can aggravate hand, wrist, or finger pain symptoms because you're continually pounding your joints and tissues. So lighten up.

❖ It's really helpful to keep everything you use regularly in easy reach. Water glass, tissues, pen, pad . . . don't be reaching for things all the time. That's just more stress on the body.

❖ If you're suffering from pain in your hands or arms, your keyboard or chair height may not be at the right level. Adjust accordingly.

❖ I avoid tired eyes, as best I can, by keeping the top of my monitor level with my eyes. If you have to, change the height of your monitor by placing some large books (never any shortage of those in a law firm!) or a sturdy box under it.

❖ Here's one that will kill you: cradling the phone between your head and shoulder. That's a sure trip—if not many—to the chiropractor, who may have you hanging from a neck brace in a doorway as a result. Get a headset! And another idea is to take your phone calls standing up. It's a good break from all that sitting down you have to do.

❖ Wear comfortable, loose clothing to work. That doesn't mean a sweatsuit, but it does mean that you should not be expected to turn up in a whalebone corset either. And kick off your shoes whenever you can!

❖ Don't neglect to introduce the issue of ergonomics as a real ongoing concern in your office. Speak to your administrator about it. Gather information. There are a lot of excellent Web sites to keep you informed, like www.ctdnews.com or www.osha.org. If your office needs a real overhaul in terms of more ergonomically favorable furniture, then you and your associates should let the powers that be know about it. It's your right.

WAR STORIES:
KEEPING ON SCHEDULE

My biggest problem was creating a schedule for my supervising attorney. He always had everything in his head and not on paper. He would come to me an hour before court and would say that this pleading had to be prepared or answered or something like that. It was all last-minute stuff all the time, and he would stand at my desk and wait for me to finish it! Nothing like a little extra pressure to get your day started.

I got him to start using a computerized schedule system. Now all of his court dates are in the computer and I know what's coming up. Usually, we sit down at the end of every week to review what's coming up for the next week and to make sure that everything is covered. Then we go over the second week so I can start working on that week. I try to keep a week ahead of the game and then just deal with the last-minute issues when they come up, which is a lot less frequently now. It makes it much easier for me, and really for him too.

CHAPTER 5

Embracing Professionalism

The issue of professionalism strikes at the heart of the paralegal community for a variety of reasons. In the first place, there is a certain degree of insecurity in the field as to whether paralegals see themselves and are seen by others as professionals altogether. Secondly, there are issues of professionalism, such as confidentiality and the unauthorized practice of law, that stand as potential mine fields for the average paralegal. Lapses of professionalism in these areas, or indeed in any areas of the practice of law, can result in severe ramifications, up to and including malpractice suits. Then, of course, professionalism is a determining factor in how well a paralegal performs his or her job. How professional are you and, hence, how valuable are you? What can you do to become more professional and more valuable? Let us hear how your colleagues in the field identify and handle these issues of professionalism.

PROFESSIONALS: ARE WE OR AREN'T WE?

❖ I believe there have been great strides, especially in the past 10 years, to make our profession more "professional." However, without standardized education or recognized utilization, we are not where we should be.

❖ The profession has depended on the good reputation of qualified paralegals to create a professional look without the aid of outside influences, such as legislation or certification. Even with the advent of two national exams, the profession has a long way to go before it is finally recognized as a stand-alone profession, rather than a "lawyer wannabe" or a "glorified secretary."

❖ I've felt a great change in the air regarding the way paralegals are seen and, in my experience, that change has really been linked to the ever-increasing importance of technology. With the advent of the technological innovations that have totally transformed your average law office, the paralegal is often the one who's the keeper of the gate. She knows the combination better than anyone else, and that gives her power and a professional gloss that may have been denied her before.

❖ I think the gauge of whether a paralegal is considered professional or not is definitely linked to the paralegal's own view of himself or herself. When a person has an absolute faith that he or she is performing to the max in a professional way, it's hard to deny that person the professional stature being sought.

❖ The feminist revolution has changed the word for paralegals, if you ask me. In the old days—and unfortunately I know because I was there—it was strictly an old boy's network. Now there are so many women partners in law firms and attorneys can no longer get away with calling their paralegal "the girl."

JUDGING YOUR WORTH

To determine whether you are, in fact, operating at a crisp professional level, you need to be able to assess your own performance, rather than wait for others to assess you.

❖ It's pretty obvious when you are being considered a really worthy member of the team. To me, one of the first indicators is the kind of assignments I'm given. Are they routinized or are they complex? Can I do them in my sleep or do they require creative thinking? If all of my assignments are essentially variations of a theme of some routine or another, I know that I'm ultimately highly replaceable . . . by a robot, perhaps.

❖ To me, it has a lot to do with whether you get an invitation to the party. You know what I mean. Are you invited to sit in on strategy sessions with the attorneys? Or is it more of a Them versus You kind of arrangement? Are the attorneys hoarding the juicy bits for themselves alone?

❖ I tend to correlate my worth with the kind of support I feel for professional growth. If I have to do all the initiating when it comes to continuing education and attending workshops and whatnot, and if I feel that there's a real resistance there—"But we like you so much better when you're working the Xerox machine!"—then I know that I stand the risk of being seriously undervalued.

❖ If I feel that "pat on the head" syndrome, I know I'm in trouble. It may be if I question a system we're using or bring up some procedural matter or even some ergonomic issue, and it's like, "Oh, yeah, sure." I know I'm not being taken seriously, and that's a red flag when it comes to how you're being valued.

❖ Money, honey. Some people like nice words and testimonials and things they can hang on their walls. I like money you can put in the bank. If I'm getting paid, preferably top-dollar, in line with other paralegals in my immediate community, than I can feel relatively secure that I'm being judged of worth. Nothing telegraphs a message more quickly and more concretely than the number of "0"s in your paycheck.

❖ Sometimes, and almost inevitably, in the life cycle of a paralegal, you're going to have some changes on the job that are not going to leave you feeling too good about things. You may find yourself buried under donkey work. You may have a change in your supervising attorney, and where you had once been doing things you really liked, like sitting in on client deposition hearings or conducting client intake interviews, suddenly you're in the land of document management and nothing else and you're ready to pull your hair out. That's the time when you have to step back and ask yourself, "What am I worth? Where should I be? How do I get there?"

Making the Most of What You Have to Offer

Once you've been able to judge your relative worth, then the issue becomes how do you let others know about it?

❖ Don't be shy. Ask for things. For instance, I learned that for me to have the kind of job satisfaction I was looking for, I needed to ask to be included in certain interface situations, like conference calls with clients. If I sat there, just looking pretty, waiting for Mr. Right to notice me, I'd never get noticed. So I did the memo bit and now, sure enough, I'm on the conference calls, and you know what? It makes me feel good. Same thing goes for being cc'ed on correspondences. When I used to see that my name was omitted on cases that I was so involved with, it would just about ruin my day. Now I'm proactive in making sure that doesn't happen.

❖ There are worse things in the world than being called pushy. Particularly if you're working in a law firm! Attorneys are just about the pushiest people you'll ever meet and, as a rule, they're not going to bat an eye if you're pushy too. In fact, they'll admire you for it.

❖ One thing you can say about paralegals is that we're an organized bunch, and so I try to bring a certain level of organization to the way I look at and assess my worth. The instrument of measurement that I like to use is the annual plan. I set myself some measurable goals, what-ever those might be, and at the end of the year I review my performance to see how far I got. Some years, I only get part way and I don't feel so great about myself. Other years I exceed my goals and then I feel like Won-der Woman.

❖ You've got to learn to ring your own bell, because you can be plenty sure that nobody's going to ring it for you. Don't hesitate to make it known when you've done some-thing valuable. If you've accrued a certain expertise in an area, advertise it throughout the firm. You've got be your own advocate for the simple reason that you'll do the job better than anyone could do it for you.

❖ I try to educate myself about new ways in which I can make myself valuable to the firm. I keep abreast of trends and new technologies and whatnot by following the Internet, reading newspapers and professional jour-nals, networking with my peers and so on. I also pay attention to what's happening in the firm. Is there an area that's growing? If so, has any of my past work been applicable? If I decide that it has been, I'll send a memo to the powers that be that points out how my prior experience would make me of use in their bailiwick.

❖ I make it a point to mentor less experienced paralegals. That way, I get to continually brush up my skills— teaching is the best kind of review there is—plus the mentoring underlines my leadership abilities and makes an impression on my supervisors.

DRESS CODE

As a professional, I have to say that I have always followed a dress code, even if it's just one of my own devising. I can remember reading somewhere that one should always dress the way your supervisor or boss dresses and not the way your peers dress, if you want to be taken seriously and get ahead. That little piece of advice has gotten me far. I am always in a skirt or dress and could be called into a conference or meeting with a client on a moment's notice. I try to look like I'm worth the client's money and to me, personally, that means no tank tops, halters, sandals, pants, and so forth.

❖ The bottom line is the bottom line. If you can save your firm money, then you will be seen as worthwhile. The more money, the more worthwhile. In other words, if you feel that you can reduce outsourcing costs by handling a project yourself, jump at it.

THE HABITS OF THE "PROFESSIONAL" PARALEGAL

What are the characteristics that employers are looking for when they hire a paralegal?

❖ If you're working in a firm that bills clients for your time, then you want to make sure that you're giving good value for the money. It's not a complicated equation. Good value means that you can handle a hefty workload in an orderly, efficient, capable way.

❖ This is so obvious it's almost ridiculous, but you'd be surprised how many paralegals I've encountered don't bother to make master documents that they can use and re-use. Instead, they start from scratch every time they need a document. Now how many hundreds of hours a year is that?

❖ Multitasking has become a buzz word in a lot of firms, and some of the paralegals I know resent it. They feel that it's a subtle way of using the whip. I don't feel that way, however. For me, returning a client's phone call while I'm doing an Internet search just makes good common sense. And the more I multitask, the sooner I can get home to my kids at night.

❖ A senior paralegal in a firm I used to work for taught me a valuable lesson. She introduced me to the idea of bio-rhythms. Some people are morning people, she explained; some people are afternoon people; and some people are evening people. (Few, if any, of us are great at all three times). If you're a morning person, like I am, you'll want to schedule your more challenging duties for that time of day, when you're bright as a pin. Then, when it's four o'clock and you're running on empty, you can do something really laid-back . . . if such a thing exists in your schedule!

❖ I've read that the average billing goal for paralegals is between 1,500 to 1,600 client-hours a year. In some firms, it's upped to around 1,800 a year. Now in my firm, if you go beyond the average, you can get a bonus. So I don't wait for my firm to set my billable goals for me. I set them for myself, and I do my best to meet them.

❖ One way that I try to embody a professional approach to my work is by eliciting responses from my supervising attorneys on a regular basis. Whenever I complete an assignment, I ask for feedback on how it was done. I also, of course, ask for and receive an annual evaluation. Even if you've been in the same place for years and you're like the indispensable right hand or whatever, you should still be getting that annual evaluation.

❖ Lists are my lifeline. Before leaving each day, I make a list of what I have to do for the next day. This simple habit organizes me and increases my work output significantly.

ARE YOU A NATURAL RESOURCE?

One of the buzzwords in the paralegal field is resourcefulness. It's a quality that supervising attorneys hope to see in the people who work for them.

❖ The way I understand it, resourcefulness is a kind of chemical reaction that occurs when you mix equal parts imagination, conscientiousness, and a streak of original thinking. It's the magic dust that differentiates you from your ordinary paralegal.

❖ Resourcefulness translates into problem-solving, and problem-solving, particularly in the context of a law practice, is worth its weight in gold.

❖ One of the most salient manifestations of resourcefulness is the ability to ask good questions. Attorneys, for the most part, know how to ask good questions, so when they spot a paralegal who can ask good questions too, it makes their pointy little ears stick up. In my experience too, attorneys hate nothing more than to have to say things twice, so by asking questions about an assignment, you obviate the need for that.

❖ I'd say resourcefulness is very connected to having a big-picture approach to things. Some people get very hung up on niggly little details and can't see the forest for the trees. A resourceful person is the opposite. A resourceful individual will be able to hack away the brush to find a route to the clearing.

❖ If you were to ask my attorney what his definition of "resourceful" would be, I can just hear him say, "Having everything at your fingertips." That's what he wants from me and that's what I give him. The sight of me rifling through papers on my desk would make him break out in hives. I need to know what's on my desk at any given moment and I need to know what's not on my desk at any given moment. So I keep a master list of files, forms and their locations. That way, I can tell him where everything is at a glance, who's checked it out, when it's coming back, and so forth.

❖ I think it's safe to say that paralegals and attorneys live in parallel universes. No attorney I know would ever think of meeting a deadline two weeks in advance. But guess what? I meet my deadlines two weeks in advance. I plan and prioritize as I need to. That's what allows me to call myself "resourceful." If I know I'll need a witness and exhibit list in two weeks' time, I want to schedule that in so I have plenty of opportunity to pull it together.

❖ The way to stay on top of things and to be thought of as resourceful is to develop a really crackerjack calendaring system. I consult my calendar a hundred times a day. I've got a whole system, with red and blue and yellow flags to alert me to what's coming up, and it's the first thing I look at when I get up in the morning and the last thing I look at when I got to bed at night.

❖ If you've ever watched that great old show *Upstairs, Downstairs,* and if you remember the way the butlers and the maids waited on the lords and the ladies, I hate to say it but there's a certain amount of that going on in the paralegal-attorney relationship. Sure, it's a profession, and nobody's expecting us to be subservient, but it is a service profession to a large extent. As such, I feel that the definition of "resourcefulness" in this context does imply thinking about and anticipating another person's needs. That's what I spend the bulk of my time doing. Does my boss have a hearing coming up? Does he need cases copied? Should I reserve the conference room? I have to ask these questions before he even thinks of them if I want to be considered a resourceful assistant.

❖ One aspect of resourcefulness translates, if you pardon my crudeness, into your ability to cover your tuchas and the tuchas of your boss. That means constant, ongoing, ever-vigilant documentation. I keep a daily diary with all of my assignment instructions, phone calls, other relevant notes, and so on.

❖ I think the willingness to work is a very obvious indicator of resourcefulness. In fact, it's so obvious that it tends to get overlooked. But the virtue of industry, which was so prized by our forefathers who started this country, still packs a punch. I make it a point always to have a project in front of me. I never look idle. If I have an hour left in the day, I don't regard it as downtime. I look it as a time for me to pick up the phone and schedule a hearing or whatever.

❖ Resourcefulness is intimately connected to initiative, and that initiative is made available to the people you work with when you, as a paralegal, present yourself as an accessible resource. That means that you show the world a positive and approachable demeanor. When people hand you an assignment, you don't sigh, grumble, roll your eyes, or give off any verbal or body language to suggest that you are less than thrilled. If you indulge in that kind of negative behavior, attorneys will find another person in the office who doesn't, and you will soon find yourself on the outside looking in.

❖ If you connect the idea of resourcefulness to a solid work ethic, that means that you bring an understanding to any assignment that it is completed within a certain timeframe. Sometimes the timeframe is a fairly generous one. Other times, it is severely compressed and that means you make yourself available to work evenings or weekends if you have to. Of course, if all your timeframes are compressed, and you have a life outside the office that you don't want to compromise, you may have to find yourself another situation.

❖ Resourcefulness is perfectly accessorized by the anticipation of need. Instead of handing documents back to your supervising attorney with the word "Here you go," you're better off handing them back with the words, "Here you go. Now would you like me to begin summarizing them?" Makes a difference, no?

❖ Your supervising attorney's idea of resourcefulness is that he or she doesn't have to pay a whole lot of attention to you. But let's imagine a situation: you need some language to prepare a document that has to be reviewed by your boss before it's filed by the deadline today. Your boss is beyond busy. Asking him where to find the language could be the straw that breaks the camel's back. So what do you do? You network. You call up another paralegal who you think might be able to help; you explain the situation; and you get the language you need. Next time, you'll help her the same way. If you can get together a network of a half-dozen such people to make up a support team for each other, you'll all be in great shape.

❖ Resourcefulness to me means keeping up to date, knowing what's happening out there in the legal world, and staying in the loop. Take the technology courses you need to remain current. Read the journals—they're filled with tips to make your life easier. Pay attention to whatever pleadings and forms cross your desk. New forms need to be copied and kept on hand for possible use in the future. Go to seminars. Be an active learner. Now that's resourceful.

❖ I've heard resourcefulness described as a lot of different things, but to me the real definition of a resourceful person is one who takes initiative and thinks creatively to produce a positive outcome. The difference between a good paralegal—one who dutifully fulfills all the duties of the job—and a great paralegal is, in fact, this resourcefulness. A great paralegal will have the ability to color outside the lines. A great paralegal will have the confidence and capacity to see new opportunities, new directions, new solutions. Maybe that means seeing a case or a transaction from the opponent's or the client's perspective. Certainly what it means is not always seeing the same thing the same way.

DEALING WITH DISASTER

Being resourceful also means being able to deal with the serious mistakes you make. Keep in mind that mistakes, even costly ones, are part of the life of a law practice. Everyone makes them. The sign of a true professional is how he or she handles those mistakes.

❖ I have made mistakes and I have seen mistakes made and, believe me, some of them have been colossal. Fortunately, I've not yet had a disaster of epic proportions, but I have friends whose mistakes were so big they almost drove them out of the profession. Their self-confidence was entirely shattered. But it shouldn't be that way. When you come down to it, handling disaster is just one other skill that a professional needs to have in place.

❖ One way to deal with disaster is to try to avoid disaster. And one way to try to avoid disaster if by being as objective as you can be about your work. You've got to step back and review your work as if you were looking at it with another person's eyes. If you do this, it's likely that the mistakes will rear their ugly little heads and you can correct them before they go on to do any real damage.

❖ This is an absolute, cardinal rule: when there's a Big Problem, step up to the plate and take the blame, if it's yours to take. Never ever try to foist the blame on somebody else. That is just really bad behavior and will do nothing other than compound the problem you've already created.

❖ Hang tough. It's a tough world out there and you've got to measure up. If you feel like an assignment is going to be the end of you, take a deep breath, say the Rosary, go in the bathroom and cry, or do whatever you have to do to muster up the fortitude to get beyond the fear. This kind of sticktoitiveness will not only be an enormous balm to your mental state, but will make your stock rise in the eyes of your employers.

❖ Ask for help when you need it. If it's practical help, go to someone you feel has the knowledge and the basic respect to share it with you. If it's emotional help you need in a bad situation, pick your friends carefully and then utilize them. That's what friends are for.

❖ I advise reading inspiring tales about people who have overcome adversity. There are so many people in the world who have had terrible luck, made terrible mistakes, and have remade themselves in wonderful ways.

❖ Tell yourself you will survive. Telling yourself this is half the battle. Berating yourself and punishing yourself is profoundly unproductive. You may be in a rough patch, but haven't you been in rough patches before and haven't you gotten beyond them?

How'm I Doin'?

Ex-Mayor Ed Koch of New York City always used to take his temperature by asking the people, "How'm I doin'?" You might want to ask that question too, whether explicitly of the people you work for or of yourself, in a kind of conscious, ongoing review of your performance in your position.

❖ Let's face it: it's not easy to accept criticism. Not for you, not for me, not for anyone. I remember the first time I got a "satisfactory" on the accuracy of my work rather than an "outstanding." I was crushed and then I was furious. "Look at me!" I wanted to shout. "I take on extra work all the time. My billable hours are top of the heap. What more do you want?" I felt like screaming at my supervisor. But then I stepped back. I allowed myself a cooling-off period of a few days. And then I came to the conclusion that my supervisor was right. My work had gotten a little sloppy here and there. What's more, my overall evaluation was outstanding, so why was I making myself crazy about the one area of improvement that had been pointed out? Now I've come to feel that the absorption of criticism and feedback is really a vital manifestation of the way a professional handles herself.

❖ I think it's natural to chafe at criticism, but, after you've had your kneejerk reaction, you might find it useful to pay attention to the message or messages that may be imbedded therein. I had an evaluation once that was decidedly less positive than what I was used to and, of course, I was upset and hurt. But, when the swelling went down, it signaled to me that I was in serious burnout. I was working in an environment where stress was the common currency, and it just wasn't good for me. I made the change to another situation where I've been very happy, but I'm grateful that I got the review in the first place and that I could read between the lines.

❖ I think you have to take any kind of review with a grain of salt. You have to trust your instincts and follow your gut. I've had reviews from people that I thought were basically very negative and counterproductive, and I didn't give those reviews any real serious attention because I didn't feel they deserved it.

❖ Formal reviews are one thing; unspoken reviews are another. Is someone who's been warm as toast to you suddenly aloof? Are you noticing a lot of closed doors with you on one side and your colleagues on the other? If these clues are mounting up, my advice is to hope for the best but prepare for the worst.

❖ Don't forget the "L" word: listen. So many people, when they receive criticism, immediately go on the defensive. They start formulating so many points to justify themselves that they don't even bother to hear the other person out. What a waste.

❖ I think it's always a good idea to have a "panel" of objective third-party members you can draw upon. If you get criticism that stings, you can go to these third parties you've confided in and you can ask for an honest, forthright appraisal. Are you as disorganized as people claim? Do you tend to have a combative attitude? Of course, it's not easy to get totally objective third parties, but, if you work at seeking them out, you should be able to find people who can serve that function for you.

❖ It's absolutely within your rights and highly recommended for you to ask pointed questions when necessary. If you feel that your workload is imbalanced compared to that of another paralegal in the office, why not say something to your supervisor like, "I'm in until 8:00 every night but I see that Fred always leaves by 5:00. Can you explain to me why this is happening?"

THE ETHICS ARENA

Ethics enters into a paralegal's work at almost every juncture. Such issues as the unauthorized practice of law (UPL), conflicts of interest, breaches of confidentiality, and unsupervised work all have their underpinnings in the realm of ethics, and can become quite complicated. These issues are central to the larger issue of a paralegal's professional conduct, and if they are not dealt with seriously and consistently, they can lead to major problems, including malpractice suits.

❖ One of the first things we learn as paralegals—well, at least one of the first things we should learn—is that paralegals, as employees of attorneys, are essentially held to the same ethical standards as their employers.

❖ Guess what, folks? Paralegals can be sued for malpractice. The same kind of civil suits brought to redress a harm caused to a client by an attorney's wrongdoing can also be brought against a paralegal. Now there's something to think about.

❖ At the very worst, a serious ethical breach can lead to a malpractice suit brought against a paralegal. Failing that, a paralegal needs to understand that a breach of client confidentiality can lead to the sanction of the supervising attorney. Which, need we point out, the supervising attorney will not be inclined to take lightly.

❖ Before considering any of the specific ethical issues that confront the paralegal, all of us in the field should be aware that most state paralegal associations publish codes designed to help paralegals navigate through the ethics shoals. The National Federation of Paralegal Associations (NFPA) publishes Informal Ethics and Disciplinary Opinions, which present scenarios outlining ethical dilemmas and their constructive resolutions. The other national organization, the National Association of Legal Assistants (NALA), has their Model Standards and Guidelines for Utilization of Legal Assistants. It is useful and important to familiarize yourself with these publications.

❖ Got an ethics question? A fast way to get an answer is to just plug onto Lexis-Nexis and dip into their Ethics Library. You'll find a full spectrum of state and national ethics opinions and codes.

❖ Because ethics issues are of such vital importance to the professional, I think it really behooves all paralegals to know where they can get fast answers. Among the Internet sites that I visit regularly are the Legal Ethics site (www.legalethics.com) where you'll find links to state associations, bar associations, and so forth.

❖ How do I make sure that I am within bounds ethically in my work as a paralegal? I start by continually educating myself about the ethical rules of my profession. I keep up with all the rules handed down by the state association and the ethical opinions of the local, state, and national lawyer associations. I attend Continuing Legal Education programs on issues of ethics. If you're not doing that sort of thing, then you're being lazy and the price of being lazy may well be that you wind up doing something you shouldn't be doing.

❖ The unfortunate truth is that you have to have something of a whistle-blower mentality when it comes to the ethics issue. Don't expect that everyone is going to be who you are. And if you think there's been an ethics breach somewhere in the system, you're really going to have to bring it to the attention of someone in charge.

❖ For me, one of the real places I've seen the ethics issue emerge over the years is around the issue of billing. I've worked in places where padding the bill or even double billing was the habit. You'd better believe I was out of there fast!

❖ I'm a notary public, and I'm appalled at the fact that other people I know who serve in this capacity will notarize documents that have not been signed in their presence. Don't let anyone bully you into doing this. It is a strict violation of code.

❖ Ultimately, ethics becomes a personal issue. Even if there are some actions or activities that fall within the boundaries of proper legal ethics, you may feel, from a personal vantage point, that your ethical guidelines are being tweaked and it may be hard for you to live with this. If the condition is chronic—if you feel that you are working with a group of habitual "tweakers"—then you might need to seek a change of venue for yourself if it is causing you distress.

CONFIDENTIALITY

Is there a concept that is more critical to professional behavior than confidentiality? The answer is no.

❖ The ability to keep client information confidential is utterly and completely central to the work of the paralegal. To be able to do so is not just a desirable thing, but it is a required thing. Unless a client consents to the disclosure of information, the attorney is ethically and legally bound to keep all information relating to the representation of the client strictly confidential. Paralegals are held to the same standard of confidentiality. That means no loose lips to your husband, your parents, your siblings, your children, your friends, or anyone else. That means no conversation about anything confidential on elevators, in hallways, or wherever anyone might be able to overhear what you're saying. That means no leaving around of papers or documents. The code of confidentiality implies that you learn a whole new way to live when you enter the field, until the issue of confidentiality becomes second nature to you.

MALPRACTICE

The bitter end of a paralegal career not followed in a scrupulously professional manner may be a malpractice suit. Among malpractice claims, the most common charge is the failure to properly calendar a matter or event. Clearly, paralegals will play an important role in creating and keeping track of a calendaring system and their work can hopefully safeguard against such claims. Another leading malpractice claim is the charges of an attorney's failure to refuse engagement. Again, paralegals can attempt to safeguard against such a claim by sending non-engagement and disengagement letters certified with a return receipt. Poor client relations are another basis for malpractice suits, and here, again, paralegals can make the difference by offering a sympathetic ear and unconditional attention to the client. In almost every instance of malpractice claims, a fine professional paralegal can head the problem off at the pass.

❖ Let's assume that every paralegal knows this, but, even so, let's restate it: A confidential name must be created for client files. This name can correlate to numeric or alphabetic sequences. No real names on files, please! Each page of each confidential document must be marked with a stamp that says "Confidential" or "Confidential-For Attorney's Eyes Only." Make sure the stamp is a different color than the document; you want it to be like a stoplight.

❖ I make sure to keep a log of all confidential documents. On the log, I note all recipients, like the opposing counsel or experts, and I have the recipients sign an acknowledgment stating that they've read the protective order and agreed to be bound by it.

❖ Guard those files with your life. Do not leave them out in the open for anyone to see. I've seen paralegals leave files on desks in libraries while they go off to the bathroom!

❖ Obviously, you don't want to leave files around in places like courthouses or libraries or any other public spaces like that. But you also have to be scrupulous about leaving them in areas of the law firm where other clients might be able to see the materials.

❖ Be completely familiar with your firm's procedure for closing a file. Know the drill around destroying documents and letters and such.

❖ I remember the days before shredders were ubiquitous. What a boon those are for the paralegal! Shred any old file that no longer needs to be retained. I, frankly, have fun getting rid of paper.

❖ One of the first places that the issue of confidentiality arises for paralegals is around correspondence that arrives for the attorney marked "confidential." So what happens if the attorney you work for is out of the country for two weeks? She's left instructions to open her mail and not to bother her unless there's an emergency. Now the letter marked "confidential" is from Mr. X, who you know is in the middle of a lawsuit. Do you open the letter? Do you hold it until your attorney returns? Do you track your attorney down on the beach in Acapulco? Obviously, what you need to do is to establish a protocol for just such a situation, and that way you will know whether or not to open such a letter.

❖ Watch yourself at parties. Drink club soda. I had a friend who went to a Christmas party, had a little too much eggnog, and she told a confidential piece of information to her friend, who was also a paralegal. Well, the friend, even though she ostensibly understood the importance of confidentiality, told her husband, and word got out. My friend was fired and it wasn't easy for her to get another job under the circumstances.

❖ There are huge issues around confidentiality and any form of electronic communications. When you're on the phone, close the door! Never have a confidential communication over a cellphone, as anyone in the vicinity with a scanner will be able to pick it up. Make it a habit, if a client calls you, to ask them if they are on a cell phone and, if so, caution the client not to divulge any confidential information while using it.

❖ Confidential portions of deposition transcripts should be marked confidential by the court reporter. The reporter can also separate out the confidential testimony and bind it separately. You can do a similar thing with videotaped depositions, where the confidential portions can be edited out of the video and placed on a separate cassette.

❖ Faxes and e-mails have obviously completely altered the lives of paralegals, but they also raise some issues around confidentiality. Make sure your faxes go to the right person and make sure you dial the right fax number. Human error, like dialing an "8" instead of a "9" is no defense. As for e-mails, you also have to be utterly scrupulous. Once you push SEND it's a done deed. So before you click on SEND, take a second to verify that the recipient is whom you intended the message to go to.

❖ I'd never send a confidential communication by e-mail. A number of state bar ethics panels have weighed in that e-mail privacy is no more susceptible to violation than an ordinary phone call is, but I just personally feel it's too risky. If I did absolutely need to send something confidential via e-mail, I'd certainly use some kind of encryption. I think I'd also want to have some kind of disclaimer in the e-mail indicating that the communication might not be secure.

SUPERVISION

Making sure that you receive adequate supervision from an attorney is another ethical issue that you, as a paralegal, must address.

❖ I factor supervision into the scope of any assignment. In other words, when I receive an assignment, I structure it. I have a planning phase, I have an execution phase, I have a personal review phase, and then I have my supervision, when I ask the attorney I work for to do the reviewing. This phase features into all of my work, and will continue in this way.

❖ Sometimes you get swept away with all the work you've got and the supervision tends to get lost in the shuffle. I safeguard against that by setting up reminders for myself specifically with regard to supervision. Otherwise put, I red-flag my calendar so that there's no way I'm going to forget what I need to do.

❖ I've worked in places where people pooh-poohed supervision and I've worked in places where the attorney and I have enjoyed a really substantive ongoing dialogue about ethics. Can you guess which situation I preferred?

❖ Let's face it: Supervision is not your attorney's favorite thing to do, so make sure you schedule it as conveniently as possible.

❖ Nag! Internalize your mother's voice and use it on your attorney. Do not stop until you get the supervision you need. If your attorney's habit is to back-burner the supervision, then he or she is not doing the job as it's meant to be done.

UNAUTHORIZED PRACTICE OF LAW (UPL)

The Unauthorized Practice of Law (UPL) is one of the most critical and sensitive issues in the paralegal world. Let us hear what your colleagues have to say about it.

❖ Do I have to say this, folks? This is serious. UPL can lead to hefty fines and even, gulp, imprisonment. And the problem is that while state statutes stipulate that only licensed attorneys can engage in the practice of law, there's a startling lack of specificity about what constitutes "the practice of law."

❖ Although there is a certain vagueness when it comes to what exactly is included under the umbrella of "practice of law," we, as paralegals, have it drummed into us some of the factors that definitely constitute "practice of law." Establishing an attorney-client relationship, setting fees, giving legal opinions or advice, representing a client in court . . . there's nothing vague about these activities and they are for attorneys only.

❖ We all know the drill, but let it be said and let's not forget it: Always, always, always introduce yourself as a paralegal or a legal assistant. Do not say, "I'm Janet Jones from Dewey, Huey, & Louie." That's a sure set-up for people to assume that you are an attorney and to ask you for legal advice.

❖ I include my title in all my correspondences. "Legal Assistant" goes right under my name. That way it's all nice and clear and out there for everyone to see. Likewise, my title is on my business card.

❖ Obviously, if you're appearing in a courtroom setting, it is mandatory that you divulge your status.

❖ A lot of clients don't really get what a paralegal is. They think you're a mini-attorney or a clone or an apprentice attorney or some such thing. Patiently and kindly explain to them how it works. All you need is a little thumbnail that you can use over and over again. And in that thumbnail, make sure you emphasize that you do not dispense legal advice.

❖ If a client comes to you asking for legal advice, here's the one bit of advice you can give him: "I'll refer you to Attorney X, Mr. Jones." End of story.

❖ Big trap? Starting a sentence with "If I were you." Whenever you hear yourself say, "If I were you, Mrs. Morgenstern," you need to put on the brakes. "If I were you" is a direct conduit into UPL.

❖ If you're working as an independent paralegal, you need to be abreast of UPL issues more than ever. There the fine line can become incredibly blurred.

War Stories:
... And More Procrastination

I used to work for an attorney who was a huge procrastinator. He would wait until 5 p.m. to start working on a brief that needed to be FedExed that night for filing the next day with the court. He had no qualms about finding the latest FedEx pickup in the city (12 midnight at O'Hare airport). The brief would require the assistance of his secretary and myself. The attorney would finally complete the brief and hand it off to us very late in the evening and go home. We were then left to assemble and copy the exhibits and prepare copies for sending to all counsel. This wasn't a problem—that was our job—but the fact that we had to wait around for him to finally finish the brief drove me crazy.

I tried a bunch of things to solve the problem. I would try and organize the file and any research materials I thought he would need and I'd have them all assembled in one spot, like a conference room. I would make a list of all the things that needed to get done for the brief and would try and make him stick to it. I would constantly be cleaning up the conference room so that we didn't lose documents we needed in the mess. I would assemble as many exhibits as possible as we chose them and would keep them off to the side so they wouldn't get lost in amongst all of his other papers. In general, I would try to keep assembling the final product (off to the side) as he worked on other parts of the brief. I would keep reorganizing the files and research materials, so that when he needed to review them again, it wouldn't take an extra two hours to find them. I would never allow him to be alone with the files for too long, because he would pull them apart and mess them up completely. I'd do all of these things and, yes, it got a little better. But did it ever get good? No. He was a procrastinator, through and through, and no matter what I did, it wasn't about to change the basic nature of his character.

Getting Organized

Head for head, paralegals are probably one of the most organized groups of people on the face of the earth. But, when it comes to organization, there is always room for improvement, particularly when your job involves setting up systems to handle a complex set of assignments. What's more, the intensity of most paralegal jobs requires equivalent organizational ability in one's personal life so that you can juggle all the demands being made on you. In this chapter, we will look at organizational tips that any paralegal can use, regardless of whether he or she is in real estate, government, litigation, or any other area of law. We will also present a wide range of helpful hints that can be integrated into your personal life to make the wheels move that much more easily.

PRIORITIZING AND TO-DO LISTS

The first order of business when it comes to organizing yourself is to develop some kind of awareness of what is urgent, what is important, and what can be delayed or even ignored. This hierarchical ranking of tasks is called *prioritizing*.

❖ Think of yourself as an emergency medical technician working in a triage operation. You've been called to the scene of an earthquake and you need to deal first with those victims who need immediate attention, followed by those who can wait a bit, and then those who can sit there reading a magazine. That's how you have to look at the work ahead of you: *immediate, in a while, maybe never.*

❖ When you are regularly getting big, demanding projects, as most paralegals do, it can become pretty overwhelming. What I do is to break the job up into segments. There might be an aspect to the job that requires phone calls, or database research, or interviewing, or filing, or whatever. If I'm feeling overwhelmed, I might start the job with one of those units that I know I can get done without my pulling my hair out. This gives me a feeling of satisfaction and relief that fuels me to go on to the next part of the job,

❖ I have to confess that I live in fear of forgetting things. Maybe it's because I entered this field as an older woman, after my kids were on their way. In fact, I'll put my memory up against the memories of most 21-year-olds I know, who, having grown up on MTV, have been conditioned not to pay any attention to anything that lasts longer than three minutes. But, still, I recognize that my brain cells are not the freshest. So I write everything down—you heard me: *everything.* As the day moves along, I keep a kind of running ledger, and whatever I do gets recorded. *Order bagel. Change ink cartridge. Check court date.* It all goes down for posterity.

❖ I don't think of myself or other people as an inexhaustible resource. In fact, I am very likely to become utterly exhausted and depleted if I or anyone else makes too many demands on me. I am an extremely hard worker, but I'm only human and know my limitations. So I've become a firm believer in what I call "my daily goal list." I get up in the morning and, while I have my coffee and croissant, I make up my list. I never have more than 10 items on it. If I can get 10 solid things done in one day, then that's a great day. Nine is less great, but still terrific. Eight is very, very good. Five or six, I don't kick myself. Three or four, I'm sleepwalking and that probably means I need to recharge with some protein, a massage, or a few days off. Less than three or four means I have the flu or my daughter's getting married on the weekend or something like that.

❖ Once I've established some priorities and I'm focusing in on the things that have to get done, I'll figure out a start date for those must-do items as well as a finish date. Sometimes there are two finish dates: the absolute one, as determined by a court date, for instance, and my own personal one, when I want to be ready with everything in advance of the court date, just to be safe.

❖ Even if there is no assigned due date to a task, I'll assign one myself, on my calendar. There's usually an implicit one anyway, so there's nothing to be gained by kidding yourself that you don't have one.

❖ I have tiers of lists in my life. Some people might think that creates just more to worry about but they're oh-so-wrong. I have my giant Master List, with my whole life on it. Then I have my daily to-do list that I take off my Master List. I also have a "palming-off" list where I'll jot down tasks that I can delegate to other people—co-workers, husband, children, any willing and able body.

❖ It's really important, when you make up your to-do list, that you group tasks in a logical and useful way. For instance, if you have to make phone calls relevant to a particular case, you'll probably want to do those all in one fell swoop. To me, it's the same kind of thinking as when you go off to the supermarket with a shopping list. You don't put down "cottage cheese" and "chicken broth" and "Liquid Plumber" and so on in one long list and then go running from one aisle to the next back to the first and what have you. You *group* the cottage cheese with the milk and the eggs and the butter and the yogurt. That's how you save time, energy, and footwork.

❖ To me, the thing about prioritizing is that nothing is set in stone. Sometimes I think a task is very important and I've put it at the top of my list, but when I'm in the middle of it, I may start to think to myself, "Hey. You know what? This isn't as important as I thought it was." You can kind of take the temperature of a task as you go along by asking yourself certain questions. Does this need the kind of attention to detail I'm bringing to it? Can somebody else help me with this or, cross my fingers, actually do it? Is this important enough to justify the amount of time I'm spending on it?

❖ There's one tip that's so obvious but a lot of people don't do it. (Including myself at times!) That is to finish one task before you go on to the next. If you've prioritized your to-do list and you've got #1 Priority, #2, and #3, don't go on to #3 in the middle of #1. That's just another way of screwing up, as far as I'm concerned.

❖ Lists without priorities make very little sense. The way that I figure out priorities is by asking myself what good thing or what bad thing could happen if I do or don't do something. If I don't file this on time, we may lose our case . . . *bad thing.* If I get this done, I can bill for it and up my measurable productivity . . . *good thing.* It's a kind of primitive mentality, but it gets me through the day.

❖ Hey, folks, here's a news flash: we're human! That means that sometimes we all get bogged down and fall behind. If that happens, and you haven't completed some of the items on your daily to-do list, fold them over to the next day's to-do list, but then don't blow that one up to 13 or 14 items. That's just a form of self-punishment and it will gain you nothing but grief. Always keep your to-do list to no more than 10 at a time.

❖ My work consists largely of subpoenaing all these med and employment records and then reading each page and preparing a date-order chronology of the person's life, which the attorney will use to take the plaintiffs' depositions. I used to put these in files but found that I sometimes forgot about them until it was too late and maybe caused an emergency for myself. Right now I have approximately 18 inches of files sitting right in front of me and there they will sit until they're done. So, as far as to-do lists go, I don't use them as much as I used to because I can see all the work that I have to do. I'll use them mostly if I'm working on a big case or if I've been out of the office for a while due to a trial or a vacation and I want to focus on all the things that will need my attention when I'm back.

❖ A to-do list is very relaxing for me, regardless of how long it becomes. Since I usually itemize every single thing that needs to be done, whether it's returning calls, drafting letters, doing research, updating charts, or what have you, it provides me with a sense of security that I'm not missing anything.

❖ I'm a firm believer in follow-up. Whenever I send out any correspondence, discovery, pleadings, or anything that requires a response, I make a follow-up note on my calendar.

ORGANIZERS

Recommending an organizer is like recommending a brand of shampoo. Do you have dry, curly hair or fine oily hair? Dyed or virgin hair? Are you out in the sun or indoors most of the time? Organizers, like shampoos, have to be chosen with one's personal needs and personality taken into account. With that caveat in place, however, let us hear what your peers have to say.

❖ I laugh when I see the apparatus, electronic and otherwise, that people use. For me, all the organizing I need can be done on a sheet of paper. I have legal pads at home and, obviously, at work, and my to-do list goes on the first available sheets of those pads. What do they cost by the gross? Less than some fancy leather-bound thing you get at some fancy department store, that's for sure, and they do the job just fine, thank you very much.

❖ I need a week-at-a-glance and a month-at-a-glance both. I've always been a very visual learner, and if I can't see the big and bigger picture, I soon feel lost.

❖ I keep everything from court dates, appointments, discovery, statues, etc. on a calendar in my computer. That way I always know what's going on and what I have to do.

❖ How can anybody these days not use an electronic organizer? Whether it's a Palm Pilot or a Handspring or any of the knockoffs, to me it's like the difference between a computer and an old Remington Rand typewriter. The way you can program in everything from birthday reminders to alarms to heaven knows what else . . . it's incredible!

❖ The attorneys in our office don't use electronic organizers, so I'm sure not going to come off looking like I'm Miss Techno Wizard. Everyone here uses an "At-a-Glance" paper calendar. I note all motions, hearings, depositions, trials, meetings, and so on—whatever the secretary dockets on the firm-wide docketing system. An e-mail is copied to me whenever she enters such dates, and I just jot it down on my calendar.

❖ I use a desk calendar, a computer calendar, and a pocket calendar. You might say I'm Miss Calendar! But, if you're like me and you can't go from here to the bathroom without checking a calendar, you better make sure that you coordinate your entries from one to the other. I've slipped up a few times and thought that what was on my desk calendar would somehow miraculously appear on my pocket calendar. It didn't and I got into deep doo-doo.

❖ While we're on the subject, don't forget your wall calendars, with erasable dry-ink markers. Having that hanging behind you is like having your own personal billboard telling you what has to be done and when.

Work Styles

Everybody has their own way of doing things. It's important to understand how you work best and to find ways to put your systems into play.

❖ I like to think of myself as a dragon slayer. I'll climb right into the pit and face the most difficult, demanding part of any job. Once I've wrestled that to the ground, everything else feels like a cinch.

❖ I take a while to warm up. I was that kid who was dipping her toe into the water when everybody else was doing belly flops off the diving board. So when it comes to penetrating a new project, I like to start easy and warm up with things I know I like to do and can do well. Research, for instance, pleases me, so I'll usually start that way and save the interviewing and phone work, which I don't like nearly so much, for later.

❖ The style that works best for me is to stick to an established routine, no matter what the project. The more closely I can follow a pattern that I'm familiar with, the more secure I feel and the more work I get done.

❖ I'm known as "The Deadline Queen" around the office. Without a deadline, I sit like a dead duck. With a deadline, I come rippingly to life. That's just the way my mind works—it's nothing to be ashamed of. But it means that I often have to go to my supervising attorney and say, "May I have a deadline, kind sir? Please?"

❖ I have to admit it: I'm compulsive. My husband says that I'd make hospital corners on his pajamas if I could. At work, I'm just as compulsive and sometimes I have to be called off a project or else I'll just keep on nitpicking until everyone's crazy. Since I know I have this problem (which is also kind of a strength, if you ask me), I've told my colleagues in the office to just wave a flag or something when they need to. It doesn't bother anyone anymore. It's kind of like a big joke.

❖ I like to work in bursts. I think of a burst as a period in which my working is very energized and focused and I get huge amounts done. Other times, when I'm not bursting, I'm treading water, but that's okay, because I get so much done in my burst periods.

❖ Let's face it—you can never be *too* organized. You might get kidded about it, but most good attorneys have way too much on their plates and they look to you for keeping the balls in the air.

MAKING THE MOST OF YOUR TIME

You know the expression, "Funny how time slips away?" Well, it's not so funny . . . particularly when your time means billing. Learning how to manage time and how to recognize and avoid time-wasters is a pressing concern of all paralegals.

❖ Some people handle interruptions better than others. I don't handle them well at all, I'm sorry to say. Interruptions interrupt my train of thought, or sometimes derail it altogether, and I just can't afford for that to happen when I've got a lot of pressure on me. But I came up with a solution. I love to needlepoint in my spare time (what spare time!) and so I made a little needlepoint pillow to hang from my office door that says "Do Not Disturb." When I need to get things done, I call upon the pillow. Now I suppose a "Do Not Disturb" sign that you take as a souvenir from some hotel would work just as well, but the needlepoint version lends a nice touch of class.

❖ I sit in a rather prominent position so I've got everyone and his brother coming by me. I angled my desk caddy corner so that I don't have to make eye contact with each passer-by. That alone has cut down on my interruptions about 20 percent.

❖ Making phone calls, even routine ones, eats up a great deal of my time, so I try to return calls when people are more inclined to be brief. From my observation of the human species, this is usually right before lunch or at the end of the day.

❖ I return all my calls in one bloc. I give myself an hour to do this. I get it done. And I never let more than one day go by without returning a phone call.

❖ I find that if I want to get things done, I have to border on rudeness at points. So if someone pops into my office with "Got a minute?" I will often shoot back, "Can it wait until this afternoon? I'm over my head right now." Even though you could call this borderline rudeness, my winsome smile will usually get me over the hump.

❖ I "give" people time. If they tell me they need to confer with me about something, I'll say, "Fine. I've got five minutes." Five good minutes of my time is nothing to sneeze at and by not keeping the exchange open-ended, I save valuable minutes all over the place.

❖ A very practical tip is this: if someone wants to meet with you about something, do it on his or her turf. It's easier for you to get in and out of that spot than for you to get somebody out of your spot.

❖ If I am interrupted, I'll always imbed a memory booster for myself in my work. Before I leave the computer, I'll stick in a reminder that can cue me when I get back. Or I might stop in mid-sentence. That way, when I sit back down to my computer, I know just where to let the other shoe drop.

❖ Interrupting is a two-way street. Ask yourself honestly how guilty you are of it. Are you a serial interrupter? Do you go around asking questions that could have waited or maybe even that never had to be asked at all?

❖ I save considerable time by having my own little law library right at my desk. I've got the Kentucky Rules of Court, the Federal Rules of Court, Taber's Cyclopedic Medical Dictionary, Nursing Drug Guide, Black's Law, and so on. Making a trip to the library every time I want to look up the definition of some medical term is a true waste of time.

❖ The worst kinds of interruptions are the ones you perpetrate on yourself. If you start one letter, then decide to start another, then get up to file something, then go back to the first letter, then make a phone call . . . well, obviously you've not worked as productively as you could have. Interrupting yourself this way is a form of procrastination and has to be curtailed. Always try to finish one task before moving on to another.

Procrastination

Scarlett O'Hara used to say, "I'll do it tomorrow, at Tara." Most of us, unfortunately, do not have that luxury. We have to do it *today*. A great deal of time and energy is sapped by procrastination. Here are some ways to identify it and to beat it.

❖ Pretty much everything on earth has its natural enemy. Rabbits get it from foxes and owls; armadillos get it from trailer-trucks on the Interstate. Productivity gets it from procrastination. No matter how well you prioritize, you may still be susceptible to the "P" word. There you are, at work on your #1 priority, and you're jumping up to go to the water cooler or the bathroom or you'll pick up the phone and tell yourself, "I'll just check in with Whomever." The way to beat procrastination is to divide tasks into manageable components. If you've got a huge caseload to organize, maybe you'll want to start with stapling or alphabetizing or something you know you can get done. Completion of any component will go a long way toward taking the sting out of procrastination.

❖ You have to think about the reasons *why* you're procrastinating. Different people procrastinate around different tasks in different ways. For instance, if the problem is that the thing you have to do is just godawful boring, you might want to try to find someone else to do it altogether, or you might want to swap with someone. Proofreading, for instance, might be one person's pleasure and another person's poison. If the problem is that the task just seems completely overwhelming, find an aspect of it that isn't and get it done. It'll make you feel good.

❖ Sometimes people procrastinate because there aren't enough deadlines built into a project. Make yourself the captain and set some arbitrary deadlines. These may spur you on enough to avoid the procrastination trap.

❖ If you're procrastinating because you simply don't know what to do, plan a course of action. It may involve calling colleagues for advice, doing research, whatever. Tell yourself you can do it!

❖ If you realize you've been procrastinating for a while and haven't come up with a good solution as to how to get out from under, you might want to do something drastic. Let's say, for instance, you've got a huge, floor-to-ceiling pile of documents that need to go somewhere. Tell the office manager that you need to be painted so that you *have* to act on the pile!

❖ Sometimes procrastination is so powerful that the best thing to do is to just succumb to it. But only for a while. Sit at your desk and stare at the assignment for 15 minutes. You'll start getting bored after 10 minutes and downright antsy after 12.

❖ I once had a situation in which I was procrastinating really seriously. My girlfriend told me what to do. She said that I should tell myself that under *no* circumstances should I allow myself to begin work on the project. Absolutely not. It was forbidden. Well, nothing's sweeter than forbidden fruit, and soon enough I was finding ways, little ways, of starting the work.

❖ Ever hear of reward therapy? When I've been procrastinating on something, I'll tell myself that if I do it, I can go out and buy myself a chocolate chip cookie dough sundae with hot fudge and caramel sauce.

❖ I think one of the underlying reasons why people procrastinate is because they're subject to perfectionism. If you think that everything has to be perfect, you may not only be intimidating others, but you may be intimidating yourself. Relax your standards a bit and you might actually see the procrastination problem disappear.

TRUE EFFICIENCY

What constitutes true efficiency? Different people have different thoughts.

❖ To me, it's all about setting up systems and basically relying on these systems to streamline and expedite your work. You shouldn't have to be *thinking* all day long about what you're *doing* all day long. The systems should make a lot of your work feel like second nature. Routines make repetitive tasks bearable. If you have to think about repetitive tasks, you'll want to jump off a roof.

❖ The key to efficiency is grouping things together so that you don't have to make too many trips. If you have to pick up your pants at the dry cleaners, figure out what's nearby and do that too. Maybe it's picking up conditioner at the hair supply place in the same mall. Same principle goes for work. Whatever you can group together, you should do so.

❖ Seek out good support whenever you can. Instead of booking flights, have a travel agent do it. If you've got to convince your boss to let you do that, so be it. Use merchants who deliver or pick up. Make your life easier whenever and wherever you can.

❖ Check your physical layout to make sure that you're husbanding your energies as best you can. Can you get to your computer, your files, your phone, and all your other vitals with a mere swivel of your chair?

❖ Pre-plan and attend to as many details as you can in advance. I always put out my clothing the night before and make sure everything's cleaned and pressed. If I know I'm going to be depositing a check the next day or I'm going to the theater, I'll have the check or the tickets in my bag the night before. There's always a million things to do on the actual day. You might as well take care of some of the little things if you can.

❖ Tell yourself that every minute counts. If you're going to lunch in five minutes, don't tell yourself, "Oh, well, I've only got five minutes. Why should I start something now?" You can make a phone call in five minutes. You can photocopy something in five minutes. In ten minutes, you can proofread something or you can make arrangements for your child's birthday party. Don't let any of that time get away from you. It'll never come back!

❖ Think creatively and try to stay a few steps ahead. For example: I work for an attorney who's great at a lot of things, but when it comes to forms, she's hopeless. How many times did I hear her say, "We're out of long distance logs" or "We're out of pleading indexes" after she's written all over the last form? So I made a master form book. Any form that comes into our office gets copied and makes it into my Form Hall of Fame notebook with its plastic protective page holders. Alphabetically arranged, of course.

In Living Color and Other "Ticklers"

Many paralegals have their own ways of tickling the memory. Here are some ideas:

❖ Do you remember that Disney song, "The world is a carousel of color?" Well, our office is a carousel of color. All of our files are in color-coded jackets—Domestic, Personal Injury, and so forth. Each file contains folders that are also color-coded, with colors for discovery, correspondence, etc. Although cases will differ from each other, the colors remain the same, i.e. discovery is always blue for any case, correspondence is always yellow, and so on.

❖ I use colored sticker dots, with each colored dot representing a week of the month. If I'm working in a blue week, and I see a file has a yellow dot on it, I know that I'm not going to have to worry about that for two more weeks.

❖ Do you remember when we were in school and we had colored tabs on our looseleafs to denote Math, Science, English, French, and so on? That worked really well, didn't it? So why shouldn't the same idea work just as well for our paralegal needs? I used to just carry around a legal pad and jot down notes and messages, but when you're working on a number of cases at the same time, it takes up valuable minutes to be going back and forth trying to find what you need. Now I use a notebook and however many cases I'm working on at any given time is however many sections I make in the notebook, with colored tabs to denote the different sections for the different cases. When someone calls me regarding one

Tips for Traveling with a Laptop

- Don't put your laptop on the conveyor belt at a metal detector to be x-rayed. Ask the security guard to search your computer manually.
- Laptops are a prime item for theft. Keep yours in a case that doesn't cry out "Laptop."
- When you're on board, keep your laptop under your seat. Don't stick it in an overhead bin where it can get thrown around.
- Always travel with extra batteries and jacks and adaptors, depending on where you are going.

case, I just let my fingers do the walking right to that section of the notebook.

❖ Color-coding is really good for managing witness and discovery files. My system works like this: I take a red-well accordion file and divide it up into sections. The blue tab denotes the witness folders; an orange tab marks oral deposition transcripts; yellow tabs show you where the medical records are; and so on.

❖ This is something that really works for me: I use my voice mail as a reminder system to myself and my attorney. I'll ring up at the end of the day and leave an item or two for my next day's to-do list. Putting messages on my attorney's voice mail is also a great way to nudge him when he gets busy. I think it's such a good trick that I've started calling my home phone answering machine to leave messages for myself. "Call Aunt Florence." "Change the bed linens" . . . whatever.

TIMESHEETS

You know the drill. You've been told time and again that you've got to keep track of your time . . . every bit of it. To do so, you need to write down—right away, before you forget—what you did. But, as you also know, this task has a habit of getting lost in the midst of a busy day. And when lots of busy days pile up, you find yourself behind the eight ball when it comes to your timesheets. What to do?

❖ In this climate we're living in, thanks to all the corporate shenanigans, you'd better believe that you and your firm could get audited for your bills. In fact, a lot of clients now are routinely sending their firms' bills to companies that specialize in auditing legal bills. Yikes! So you had better make sure that you have clearly identified the exact work that you've performed, that you have explained why the work was necessary with regard to the case, and that you haven't disclosed anything in this record-keeping that could be construed as privileged information.

❖ Just be careful because sloppiness can catch up with you in a truly bad way. I had a friend, for instance, whose firm was audited for a legal bill and one of her notes said that she had "talked to Gus Shaw." Now by the time the audit happened, she had no idea who the heck Gus Shaw was and she couldn't find a record of him anywhere. Finally, she was able to discover that he was a metallurgist who had been used as an expert on the environmental case she had worked on, and if she had just put down "Gus Shaw, metallurgist" she would have saved herself days of work!

❖ Always use first and last names in your timesheets, preceded by a Mr. or Ms. "Spoke with Ms. Jane Evans," for instance. You don't want any plain Janes or Toms and Dicks and Harrys in your timesheets.

❖ You really have to be scrupulous about not disclosing any privileged information, even obliquely, in your timesheets. Never, for instance, should you suggest or indicate any kind of legal conclusions, opinions, or anything of the sort.

❖ Ever play poker? First rule is not to show your hand. You want to make sure you don't do this in your timesheet notations either. For example, you don't want to write something like, "Work on licensing agreement between Macy's and Gimbel's as a means to avoid cross-complaint." This shows too much of your strategy and if it falls into the wrong hands, it's bye-bye strategy.

❖ You'd better be darned good at getting down time entries. If your entries are vague or sloppy, your supervising attorney is likely to red pencil them, meaning less in your pocket and less evidence of your overall measurable productivity.

❖ Fuzzy timesheet entries lead to fuzzy billing which leads to slow paying. End of story.

❖ One place where you're really going to have problems with sloppy timesheet entries is if the work you're performing for the client is being paid through insurance coverage. The claims adjuster will pounce on anything that looks nebulous and you may never see your money.

❖ A very unpleasant situation may arise if your supervising attorney has to rewrite your timesheet entries in the context of a pre-bill or a billing memorandum. Busy attorneys do not look kindly of becoming the editor for paralegals who haven't gotten the timesheet bit down yet.

❖ As soon as you start working in a new situation, make a study of how the timesheets are handled there. Ask for samples and confer with whomever to find out what the customs of that particular culture are. Nag people for feedback on your timesheets. Better to nag than to be rapped on the knuckles—or, worse yet, to have your revenues scaled down—later on.

TRAVEL

Paralegals are often called upon to travel for trials, filings, discovery, or any number of other reasons. Some organizing tips can make these business travels so much easier.

❖ If you travel a lot, keep a master list of all your travel needs, with everything on it from alarm clock to shampoo, moisturizer, money belt, what have you. Before you take off on a trip, check off the items on your checklist.

❖ When you're packing your suitcase, write down on a running list everything that you put into it. That way, if your luggage is lost, you'll know what was in it.

❖ Get a good map and guide to where you're going *before* you get there. Your car rental agency may be all out of maps, so don't get stuck.

❖ Travel light, whatever you do. Less is more. If you don't have to deal with anything but a carry-on, you'll be way ahead of the game. You'll never have to deal with long waits at the carousel or running after an airline for lost luggage.

❖ I always bring my own pillow with me when I travel. A stiff neck sets my productivity back hugely. Also, I like to bring a nightlight with me. Some hotel rooms are pitch-black and I don't want to bang up a shin trying to find my way in the dark.

❖ Keep all your receipts in one place if you're planning to put in for reimbursement.

❖ Always carry an extra pair of eyeglasses with you, or at least your prescription.

❖ If the hotel you're staying at has a dedicated business floor, do your best to reserve a room there. Not only will you get rooms with dual telephone/modem lines, fax machines, and free local calling, but you're more likely to be insulated from the sounds of crying babies and screaming rock bands.

❖ Most hotels hit you up big-time for using their fax machine. Better to go to a nearby store or business center.

. . . And on the Personal Side

No matter how organized you are at work, you may let things slide at home. It's important to correct this imbalance, because, ultimately, lack of organization at home may affect your performance at work. Of course, there are far too many ideas for us to talk about with regard to your homefront issues, but here are some useful tips to get you started.

❖ Here's a trick of mine. When I feel badly cluttered at home, I make believe I'm moving and I systematically go through each room of my house, deciding what does and what doesn't deserve to go into a box.

❖ Cardinal rule: keys, glasses, wallet, mail all go in the same place every single day. Never deviate from the routine. That way you will buy yourself countless hours where you're *not* looking for your keys, wallet, glasses, mail!

❖ Keep a wastebasket in every room. If you have to walk to another room to throw something away, chances are you won't.

❖ I make it a rule never to leave a room without picking up something that belongs somewhere else and depositing it there. You'd think I'd run out of things that belong somewhere else, but somehow I never do.

❖ All of us accumulate too much *stuff* and you have to be ruthless about getting rid of it. Take your refrigerator, for instance. Do you really need that half-full jar of pickled cocktail onions? What's the last time you made a martini with a pickled cocktail onion in it? Do you even *like* pickled cocktail onions? The same rule can be applied throughout your house. Do you really need the porcelain life-sized schnauzer that your Aunt Gladys gave you for Christmas? (She's gone now, poor thing, so if you give it to Goodwill she'll never know). Train a discerning eye all over your house and get rid of clutter!

❖ Get yourself off mailing lists. If you receive catalogs from companies that you're not interested in, call them up immediately and ask to be removed from their list. Same for e-mail junk.

❖ Magazines were the bane of my existence. They'd stack up and make me feel guilty about not having read them. Then a friend gave me a great idea. He said I should get a redwell folder and clip any articles from the magazines that interested me, stick them in the folder, and read them as I could. I found that many of my magazines didn't have more than one or two things in them that interested me. This has saved me a lot of space and a lot of guilt!

❖ Kids make clutter way beyond anything you could imagine. To combat it, I've introduced a new "tradition" in our household. Each year, before Christmas, I have the kids go through their things and we make piles of toys and books and clothes that we're not interested in anymore but that would be good for other people. We "make room for Christmas" this way and the kids wind up feeling good about the giving act too.

❖ I made a decision some time ago to throw away any broken item, anything that was missing one leg or one piece, with the idea that somehow I would find a replacement or have it mended. I never get around to stuff like that, it makes me sad to see these things lying around, and life's altogether too short for that. As for single earrings . . . I give them to my son!

❖ I'd like to celebrate the messy closet. The Fibber McGee closet. The one where you throw things when you have no idea what to do with them. Every house should have one, and no one should ever feel guilty about it.

JUGGLING WORK AND FAMILY

Here is another huge issue in the lives of many paralegals, touching on the organizational but obviously going beyond that. Its is much too large for us to try to cover here in any depth, but we wouldn't want to leave this chapter without touching on it and offering a few thoughts.

❖ This is an issue that has torn at me for years now. It's a very big conflict. All I can say is that the way to begin dealing with it is to identify your goals. What are your professional goals? What are your personal goals? How do they interface? Can you be all things to all people?

Should you even try? Once you've identified these goals—and you may even need the help of a professional counselor in doing so—then you have to try to stick to them.

❖ I would never try to plan out my career without the input of my family. We collaborate on my career goals. I might say to my kids, "I can go for this job, but it will mean that you two will have to pick up a lot more of the slack around here. How do you feel about it?" Sometimes, they'll say yes, sometimes no. It depends where they're at in their lives, and I have to listen to them and respect where they're at in their lives.

❖ End your day in the office and don't make a habit of bringing work home with you. Too many Americans in the 21st century believe that there's something wrong with them if they're not working day and night. That's baloney. In Europe, people get a whole month of vacation and the whole family goes off to the beach to rediscover each other. Here, in America, we worship the cult of the "workaholic" and a week here and a week there is supposed to be a regenerating holiday? Come on!

❖ I segregate. When I'm at work, I'm at work and I don't devote any time other than is absolutely necessary to my personal agenda. I don't make calls to my mother or girlfriends or anything like that. That way, I get more done at work and so I don't have to bring work home with me.

❖ I make no bones to my attorney about what my personal needs are. If my kid is starring in a play at school, I give my attorney ample notice and I tell him that, under no circumstances, will I be available to stay late that night or meet any unusual morning deadlines. He knows I won't budge on certain matters, and I have to say that I've never had a problem.

War Stories:
Public Offender

I would find it really troubling when my attorney would tell me about my work in my "cubicle dwelling" where the entire office could hear. It might be about the quality of the work I did, and if it was negative, I felt it made me look stupid to the other secretaries and paralegals. I put up with it for the first two months and then finally said, in hushed tones, "Could you please keep it down so that the whole office doesn't think I'm an idiot?" That got through to her.

I have three sons, and, as a single mom, I know how multi-tasked I am and how well I do at holding it all together. This is my mantra to myself when things get crazy in the office. I know I can manage to do more around here than most anyone and I can do it better. Mind you, however, I say these things only to myself, not to the attorneys.

CHAPTER 7

Research, Writing, and Technology

For many paralegals, research and writing is dessert. This is the aspect of the job that they love. For others, of course, research and writing are a stretch, a hurdle, or even something worse. This chapter presents a wide range of tips from your fellow paralegals regarding everything from e-mail etiquette to interviewing to editing and more.

RESEARCH

Research is obviously a very big part of a paralegal's life. Let us break down this area a bit and look at some of its components more closely.

General Research Tips

The ability to put your hands on facts and information almost immediately will earn you respect from attorneys and clients alike. Here are some thoughts about how to become such an expert:

❖ The place to start is at the beginning. You have to become thoroughly versed in what's out there. There are so many directories and sources; the challenge is to get to know them and to develop a sense of what you can get out of each.

❖ As is true in so many areas of life, the key to successful legal research is organization. I keep a checklist of resources and, as I search for case law, I'll go down my list and check off which sources I've used and which I have pending.

❖ Nowadays we go to the supermarket and we buy our meat all wrapped up in plastic in a Styrofoam tray. But my grandmother always used to say that if you wanted to get a really good cut of meat, you had to know the butcher well. You had to say, "How's the wife, Mr. Schultz?" if you wanted something special. The same, more or less, is true in law. If you want to be able to get the information you need quickly, you have to develop a relationship with the law librarian or the people over at the research service or the document retrieval service. Even though it may feel at times like the whole world is online, the human factor still counts for a lot.

❖ Every paralegal should know about the Federal Register, but a lot don't. The Federal Register is a kind of clearinghouse for information about federal regulations and activities. Whenever a piece of proposed regulation is published, or there are announcements about comment periods or final regulations, the name and number of the official responsible for the action is included in the Register. You'll be able to get the phone numbers of these people, and, nine times out of ten, you can actually get them on the line and they'll be happy to talk to you.

❖ I proposed in our office that we get a toll-free 800 number for our fax line, so that government agencies wouldn't have to think about any budgetary constraints when faxing us the documents we asked for.

❖ Does everyone know about the Law Digest that sits at the back of the Martindale-Hubbell Directory? It gives you brief digests of significant laws in every state and country. This information is updated regularly and I've found it very reliable.

❖ When doing research on the Internet, it's useful to compile and bookmark a list of good sites. You don't want to have to start from scratch every time you go researching.

❖ I know paralegals who, if they can't find what they need in a book or a database, will sit there scratching their heads or maybe give up altogether. Now that's crazy. Didn't these people ever hear of picking up a phone? You can get a court, a library, or a government agency on the line and you can be Nancy Drew to your heart's content.

TIPS FOR WORKING WITH A DOCUMENT SEARCH COMPANY

- Start out by feeding *them* information, rather than the other way around. Try to be precise about what you're looking for. If you've got a case or even a court name, better yet. The more you narrow the parameters, the faster and cheaper they'll work.
- Make sure to establish a budget at the point of contact. Are you in a rush? That will cost you. Overnighting documents, for instance, will be cheaper than faxing them, so take that into account. Whatever you do, you don't want to be surprised by the bill at the end.
- You weren't really looking for 1,500 pages of document, were you? If not, then you might be in for a shock unless you set a page limitation with the company first. Don't just tell them to "copy a case!"

CITATION CHECKING IN WESTLAW®

Consider these useful tips when using KeyCite®:

- A red flag signifies that the case has been reversed or overruled.
- A yellow flag indicates that a case that has been questioned and should be checked.
- Do not cite a case without verifying that it is still good law.

❖ If you come up against a dead end in your research, you might want to consider using a document retrieval service. They'll be able to get you almost anything you need, whether it's a transcript of a hearing, documents issued by a federal agency, or what have you. Really—you wouldn't believe what these services can get a hold of.

Case Law Research

Case law lies at the heart of all legal research. Cases help you understand how to use cross-examination, expert witnesses, forensics, charts, videos . . . you name it. Cases *are* law, so any paralegal worth his or her salt really ought to know how to find what is needed.

❖ I create a case index and make a list for each case I locate. My choice is to use 3 × 5 index cards. Okay, so it's not the most high-tech approach in the world, but you know what? It works beautifully for me. I stick the cards in my little card case and I take them to the library and I know just what I've got. Sometimes, if I feel like it, I'll add additional information to the cards, like the jurisdiction, the main legal issue of the case, references to other cases, and so forth.

❖ It's really important to find the right keywords when doing your case law research. Some people find that frustrating and get quickly stumped. Me, I'm the kind of person whose idea of a perfect Sunday morning is a cup of coffee and the hardest crossword puzzle I can find. So keyword challenges are manna for me. Oh, and one more thing: keep a running list of keywords as a reference. You'll want to go back and consult them, instead of reinventing the wheel every time.

❖ Keep in mind that just because you've found a case that looks relevant, it may not really be so. It may have been reversed on appeal, for instance. Or the statute on which the decision was made may have been repealed or amended. So don't ever take validity for granted. Conduct a historical review of each case, using Westlaw® or Lexis-Nexis®. Inaccurate research can cause you not only to lose a case, but opens you up to a possible malpractice suit.

Interviewing

We situate interviewing within the research area, because gathering information by interview is, after all, a form of research, is it not? Your interviewing prowess will benefit from developing a set of task-specific skills, which, fortunately, can be mastered by most people.

❖ When I first started interviewing people, and this goes back a while, I'd have to say I was a disaster. Invariably, I'd come away from an interview realizing that I had forgotten to ask any number of questions that were critical. I'd have to call up the person on the phone, and it was embarrassing.

❖ For any interview you do, even something as basic as a client intake interview, you should pull together a summary sheet that your attorney reviews before you actually do the interview.

❖ You have to do your homework, boys and girls. It's like when you watch a television talk show. Some of the hosts have really brushed up on who their guests are and what they've written or done lately, and the interview is good. Others have been too busy getting their hair blow-dried and so, without having done the homework, they'll ask questions that are vague or toothless. Don't let that happen to you. Before you ever sit down with a witness, make sure you understand the facts of the case. Review the file thoroughly. Maybe you want to get a map of the relevant area or, better yet, you might even want to drive it.

❖ Write out your list of questions! Maybe there are some people in the world who can go the interview route ad hoc and unrehearsed, but I'm not one of them and chances are neither are you. I write all my questions at the front of my pad, clearly numbered in sequence, and then I number the responses to correlate to the questions. Before I end an interview, I actually say, "May I just take a moment to review my questions one more time?" And that's how I make sure I haven't left out anything important.

❖ Try to inject a human feeling into your interaction with the person you're interviewing. Use the person's name here and there. If the interview is done in the flesh, rather than over the phone, use a conference room. Don't have the person on one side of the desk with you on the other, like you're Sgt. Joe Friday from *Dragnet* or whatever. Offer coffee or a soft drink. Smile. And then smile again . . .

❖ If you've got photos or maps, bring them along to the interview. Visual prompts can jar the memory of an interviewee more than words possibly can.

❖ Before you even begin the interview, think about how you're going to address the other person. I'm kind of formal myself, and one of my pet peeves is if I call up an airline or a catalog company or whatever to place an order, and the person on the other line calls me "Margaret." How did I become Margaret to them all of a sudden? So when I interview someone, I always err on the side of formality, using Mr. or Mrs., particularly if there's an age difference or any cultural considerations. If you're unsure about the formality level, it's perfectly

---

Tape-Recording Interviews

Here are a few useful pointers to keep in mind when tape-recording an interview:

- Test the recorder before the interview to make sure it is functioning correctly.
- Start the tape with a prepared introductory statement that gives the name of the person being interviewed; the date, time, and location of the interview; the name of the case; and any other information you deem relevant.
- Ask the person being interviewed to state his or her name and to spell it into the recorder.
- Ask the person being interviewed for permission to tape-record the interview. Make sure that the permission is heard on the recording.
- Ask any other parties present at the interview to state and spell their names into the recorder.
- Always come prepared with extra tapes and batteries.
- Immediately label a tape as you remove it from the recorder.
- If you have used more than one tape for an interview, label which number the tape is and include on the label how many tapes altogether comprise the interview.

---

fine to ask. No one will mind if you say, "May I call you Jim?" . . . unless their name's not Jim, that is.

❖ Don't forget to telegraph your messages with some persuasive body language. Encouraging nods, sympathetic frowns, a cocked head . . . these will often elicit responses that words cannot extract. Some verbal support, like "Uh-huh" or a sympathetic "Tsk," can also help things move along. By the same token, negative body language, like looking at your watch or yawning, gives out clear and sometimes interview-ending messages.

❖ Listen! Listen! Listen! Too many times when people are interviewing other people, they're thinking about their next question instead of listening to the response to the question asked.

❖ I've invariably found that the most powerful single tool in an interview is silence. When a person has given you a response, and it's not everything you wished it to be, if you just don't rush in to fill the void with your words, it's altogether likely that the interviewee will feel compelled to keep talking. Try it sometime!

❖ Some people just blather and drone, blather and drone, and you have to develop a way to stop them. What I do is say, "Can we just hold that thought for a second while I jot this down?" It's usually enough to get them off their deadly course . . . until they find another deadly course.

❖ Reflect the words back to the interviewee as you go along. That way the person can amend or elaborate as necessary.

❖ Sometimes tape-recording an interview is essential, but, if it isn't, it's not always the best route. For one thing, a recorder might intimidate a subject. For another, you'll be left with a hefty document to transcribe. If you decide that handwritten note-taking will do the trick, there are some good hints to keep in mind. Obviously, you have to write fast, so what I do is I create my own shorthand. I use a + sign for "and," for instance. I might only write the consonants for certain words, like "lg brkn in accdnt." This means "leg broken in an accident." But of course you'll have to write this out immediately following the interview so you won't forget what your shorthand was all about.

❖ A clever thing to do when you're writing down notes as you interview someone is to ask them a question that you don't really need to have an answer to, just to buy time to write down the answer from the previous important question. Like, "Who does your hair?" (Only kidding!)

❖ It's important to understand the construction and sense behind different types of questions. For instance, you don't want to join two questions together. You don't want to say, "How did you and your wife meet and what do you think drove you apart?" That won't get you anywhere. Similarly, it's important to ask a global question at the end of the interview. "Is there anything we haven't touched on that you think I should know?" for instance. These types of questions are very important.

WRITING

Writing plays a vital role in the legal profession, for paralegals as well as attorneys. Whether it is interrogatories, memos, demand letters, or any number of other forms, you will surely be called upon in your career as a writer to put pen to paper . . . or finger to CUT and PASTE.

General Writing Tips

All writers, no matter what their level of proficiency, are works in progress. As difficult as writing can be, the good news is that we can all get better if we work at it. Here are some tips from those who have.

- ❖ Always use natural, plain English. Steer clear of legalese—it's deadly. Keep in mind that your clients are not themselves attorneys and so there is no reason why they should even begin to understand the baroque turns of phrases that have marked this profession for so long. In fact, it is my opinion that one of the reasons why lawyers are so generally unpopular with lay people is because of this very language.

- ❖ Follow the leader. If you're unsure about how to write something, get a good sample and adapt your own piece accordingly. Your firm's files are probably full of good writing samples.

- ❖ You may be writing something worthy of a Pulitzer Prize, but if it's not done by the due date, it's not going to win any awards and you're going to be in serious hot water. Check your court dates regularly to make sure you're on the beam.

- ❖ I think the best thing you can do to improve your writing is to read out loud whatever you've written. Of course, it would be ideal to be able to read it to another person, but there are few people in this world so saint-like that they will listen to your briefs to make sure they're good.

- ❖ I like to get my documents done several days ahead of time and then let them sit. You know how it's good to make lasagna a few days ahead of time so all the flavors can develop? That's the way it is with what you write. You get a different view of something if you can come back to it after a few days.

- ❖ You know the old joke, "How do you get to Carnegie Hall? Rehearse, rehearse, rehearse?" Well, you could adapt that to, "How do you achieve good legal writing? Rewrite, rewrite, rewrite." Rewriting is the most important part of writing, if you ask me, and I can still remember the old days when we used carbon sets and typewriters. Today, with the touch of a button, you can cut and paste and really revel in the joy of rewriting, so there are no excuses not to do it.

❖ When you're rewriting and revising, keep a checklist handy of key questions to ask yourself. Is the piece well-organized? Does it flow? Is the language clear and plain and accessible to all readers, not just people in the field? Are there transitions that make it easy for you to move from one section of the piece to another? What can you cut out? What have you repeated? Where are the redundancies? Have you checked the citations and their form?

❖ Someone could have some basic talent for sculpting, but if that person never studied anatomy, you wouldn't expect to see an understanding of the human form in the sculpture. Similarly, you could be an inherently good writer, but if you don't understand or really know the form of basic memoranda and briefs, it's not going to do you a lot of good. Memoranda are structured as follows: issue, short answer, statement of facts, discussion, conclusion. Briefs have this form: question, statement of fact, argument, conclusion. Paralegals need to understand the basics of these writing forms and then they can pay attention to issues of style.

❖ Figure out what time of day is best for you to write, and do it then. If you're a morning writer, don't try to write at midnight.

❖ J.K. Rowling wrote her first Harry Potter book sitting in a café. I've found that I do some of my best writing when I take my laptop to the Starbucks down the street. I like the buzz around me. The absolute silence of a library makes me nervous.

❖ I do timed writing spells. I tell myself that I will write for twenty minutes without getting up. Twenty minutes of uninterrupted writing can feel like two hours, but I find that it gets the job done for me. And there's no checking of e-mail during those 20 minutes either!

❖ One of the most important parts of the writing process is the pre-writing. That's the part before you even get started. Make sure you've listened carefully to your instructions and ask any questions right at the beginning. Make sure you understand format issues as well as content issues. Check with your supervisor regarding format if you have any doubts.

❖ Anyone who sits down to write something needs to understand that there will be several, if not many, drafts. Shakespeare didn't get it right the first time he put it down on paper, so why should you? Use a large, bold font on your early drafts so the mistakes will pop out for you. And, of course, double-space your drafts so you can pencil-edit between the lines if you care to.

❖ What's the goal of the first draft? To put the research and analysis into nice, organized sentences and paragraphs. Go for structure in the first draft. You can do your polishing later. It's best not to polish as you go along. You lose the big picture that way.

❖ Sometimes you may become snagged on a certain section of what you're writing. Don't get hung up there. Just leave it and go on to another section. You can come back to the problem section after you've had a victory elsewhere in the piece.

❖ This probably goes without saying, but better say it anyway. Use your spell-check. Use your grammar-check. That's what they're there for.

❖ Proofreading is so important and it's hard to do it for yourself. I have a buddy system with another paralegal. We proofread all of each other's writing. It's great!

❖ I keep a file of constructions, paragraphs, and passages that I've written and that I think are good. Then I recycle them as often as I can.

❖ I try to read a lot of journals and to pay attention to what's being written there. The good writing I see in these journals inspires me to do some of my own good writing.

❖ Always identify yourself as a paralegal in your writings! Don't let people think you're giving them legal advice.

Good Writing Style

Good clean writing is something all of us should aspire to. Here's how:

❖ I'm often complimented on my writing style and my secret, as far as I can see, is so simple that it's almost

Nonsexist Titles for Various Occupations

Don't use	Do use
authoress	author
chairman	chairperson, chair
fireman	firefighter
foreman	supervisor
policeman	police officer
postman	mail carrier
sculptress	sculptor
stewardess, steward	flight attendant
workman	worker

embarrassing. I keep my sentences short. But, of course, some of my sentences are a little more complex than others, because having all short sentences does not make for a satisfying reading experience either.

❖ Lists and bullets are useful. They're easier to read and to refer to than long sentences full of commas.

❖ Direct address makes a document feel more immediate for the reader. So if I'm writing something that is supposed to provide information for the client, I refer to the client as "you" and to the firm as "we."

❖ Be consistent in your references. Don't refer to a "house" in one paragraph, a "home" in the next, and a "residence" or "abode" in those that follow. Come up with one term—let's say "home" —and use it throughout. That way, the reader doesn't have to wonder whether there are varied nuances imbedded in these words that he may not fully understand.

❖ Plain English, please—first and always. Instead of "henceforward" (as if anyone in the real world would use such a word!), how about a nice, normal phrase like "from now on." And isn't it always better to say "whatever" than "whatsoever or "even if" than "notwithstanding"? If you have to establish your authority as a legal expert by using these arcane legal expressions, than you're doing something wrong

Plain English

Consider the list below and make the following substitutions in your writing:

Legalese	Plain English
afford an opportunity	allow
ascertain	find out
bestow	give
comply with	follow
discharge	carry out
due to the fact that	because
forthwith	now
in lieu of	instead of
in some instances	sometimes
in the absence of	without
in the course of	while
in the event of	if
in view of the fact that	because
irrespective of	despite
is of the opinion	thinks
not later than	by
prior to	before
pursuant to	because of
said "witness"	the "witness"
subsequent to	after
until such time	until

Get the idea?

❖ One thing that we probably all learned back in our high school writing classes, but may have forgotten under the influence of all the bad legal writing we've been exposed to, is to use the active voice rather than the passive voice. A passive construction is something like, "The man was hit by the car on Sepulveda Boulevard." The active voice is, "The car hit the man on Sepulveda Boulevard." As you would expect, writing in an active voice is livelier and usually much clearer.

❖ Avoid awkward habits like turning verbs into nouns. For instance, try not to say, "He will make a delivery of the letter tomorrow." Instead, just be direct and say, "He will deliver the letter tomorrow."

Avoiding Plagiarism

Plagiarism, by which one copies another's work without acknowledgment, is a serious offense, and writers can indulge in it unconsciously. You might take down language from another document word-for-word, then neglect to paraphrase it or directly attribute it when writing your own brief, thus opening up yourself and your employer to charges of copyright infringement.

❖ To guard myself against plagiarism, I always make a point of including quotation marks around things I write down verbatim and I jot down the source of a quotation when I'm copying somebody's else's words.

❖ Once you get the hang of it, writing in plain English is so much easier than writing in legalese. And so much more appreciated! But you won't learn how to do this overnight. It will take you a while, maybe even a full year or more, to rid yourself of that legalese voice. Practice by revising documents or letters that you think are full of the kind of language that nobody but a lawyer would understand. Once you get going, you might even have fun with this kind of assignment. We know an office where they have a writing contest every year. Everyone tries to write a plain English draft of the same document—attorneys, paralegals, secretaries—and the entries are judged by an impartial panel. The winner—the person who had written the clearest and most engaging version of what had been a dead and deadly document—wins two tickets to a Knicks game.

Plain English

To learn more about plain English, check out these Internet resources:

A Plain English Handbook
http://www.sec.gov/news/extra/handbook.htm
Plain English Campaign
http://www.plainenglish.co.uk/
The Plain Language Association International
http://plainlanguagenetwork.org
Plain Language Action Network
http://204.254.113.225/main.htm

❖ Strive for nonsexist language. Watch your pronouns. When speaking generally, don't use the word "he." For instance, if you say "a paralegal should always continue his education," you will want to change that to something non-gender specific, like "a paralegal should always subscribe to continuing education" or use a plural if you can, as in "Paralegals should always continue their education." You could also use "his" or "her," as in "A paralegal should always continue his or her education," but, as you can see, this can become cumbersome. Avoid the use of s/he. It's awkward and tends to stop readers in their tracks.

❖ As we all probably know by now, "Ms." is the preferred title for women, as it does not gratuitously disclose marital status.

The Legal Memorandum

One of the most important forms for a paralegal to master is the legal memo.

❖ Memos have to be written well and have to grab the interest of the reader. Otherwise, they tend to get overlooked, which means that your time has been wasted. The expectation when you write a memo is that it may be used at a later time as an official court document, so better make it good.

❖ Just as a newspaper reporter has to write a good "lead" for an article, so you have to write a good first line to capture your reader's attention. Make sure you use the active voice rather than a passive one, and pick some nice, muscular verbs to get your point across.

❖ Another trick: if, for some reason, you want to de-emphasize a point (let's say there's a fact in there that you'd like to obscure a bit), choose the passive voice. The passive voice makes things kind of fade into the woodwork, which, for the purposes of obfuscation, is exactly what you're looking for.

❖ Arrange your facts in order of importance. Some people feel hidebound to present facts chronologically. Don't buy into that. Arrange your facts so that the ones you want people to register are upfront and on top.

❖ Always, always, always note the source of your facts. You don't want to go back and have to find them all over again. If you're asked to include citations, make sure that everything is Shepardized®.

❖ Does your case law support your client's position or not? Keep a checklist of your findings.

❖ Ideally, the memo should be self-contained. The reader should not have to refer to the case file in order to come away with an understanding of the issues, the facts, or the analysis of the piece.

❖ The person who mentored me when it came to writing internal legal memoranda drove some basic points into my brain. I was always to conduct a counteranalysis, for example. I was always to discuss how the rule of law applied to the issue and facts of the client's case. And, most important of all, she said, was that I shouldn't feel compelled to come to a definite conclusion as to how the law applied. Sometimes the answer just isn't there and you don't have to act like you have all the answers.

❖ In preparing external legal memoranda, you should always check the court rules with regard to format and length. For instance, some courts may not require you to have a table of contents or an argument summary.

Technology

Technology is the joy of some people, the bane of others. For paralegals, technology should be valued, for it has made life so much easier for everyone in this profession. Still, the relationship between human and machine may always be, at best, an uneasy one. Let us hear what others in the field have to say about this subject.

❖ Are you kidding? I love technology! Word processing has turned me into a hugely better writer. Computerized forms can be downloaded at the touch of a button. Database management means that we don't have to search through hundreds of boxes of documents like we used to in the old days. Online databases bring legal research into an entirely new realm. What's not to love?

❖ I think the Internet is one of the greatest things ever invented. It's one of the Seven Wonders of the World!

My goodness, Mapquest alone would make me love it. Any time I ever have to drive anywhere, I just log on to http://www.mapquest.com and I have the perfect directions!

❖ Some paralegals fear that technology will obviate the need for them. That's foolish. Technology just opens more doors for paralegals. Many paralegals now market themselves as Internet specialists, while others have become expert at electronic evidence.

❖ My aptitude for technology and the familiarity I have with the technological systems we use in our office has made me an indispensable person, if I do say so myself. I think I would always have been highly considered as a paralegal, in any day and age, because I'm organized and careful and smart. But the knack I have for technology means that I'm really in the right place at the right time because so much of what happens in law now is linked to technology.

❖ I'm not that ancient, but I can remember the days before e-mail. Can you imagine a world without e-mail? Even though I was without it for most of my life, I can hardly remember a time when we didn't have it. Before the advent of the computer, we paralegals were like people in the Stone Age, using clubs and sharpened bits of stone and shells to get our work done.

❖ My status in the firm has been elevated significantly since I took it upon myself to become the technologically-educated one around here. I'm always going to workshops and seminars, and now I'm the "go-to" person when we have to make decisions about what kind of equipment to buy or upgrade.

BACK UP, PEOPLE!

Power failures will occur. Surge protectors help but don't offer you absolute protection. The only real protection against loss of work is regular and scrupulous backing up of your files. A crash-saving program such as Norton Utilities will also help recover lost data.

❖ If you're a paralegal today who doesn't know diddly-squat about electronic information retrieval, electronic filings, and online research, then you're going to be like those dinosaurs who got stuck in the tarry mud pits of LaBrea. You're going to be left behind while others who have put in the time and work take the reins.

❖ I'd just like to go on record as saying that some of the junior paralegals in our firm who are computer-savvy think they're the greatest thing since sliced bread and those of us who don't always know our way around that world are basically useless antiques waiting to be dispatched to the glue factory. Let me just point out that a paralegal needs lots of knowledge and smarts in areas that have *nothing* to do with technology, so I wish those kids would stop acting so uppity.

❖ Take heart: just about anyone can become educated with regard to technology. Most of what you have to learn is really quite user-friendly. Sure, it may represent a whole new world to you, but what've you got against a whole new world? Is the world you've been living in so perfect that you can't stand to see some change?

❖ In order to master new technology, you might have to turn your meter off, or at least slow it down a bit, with regard to your billable hours. You can't do it all, and your choice for the moment may just have to be that you're going on a learning curve. Once you've made the trip, you can get your stride back and your billing will probably be better than it ever was, because one thing about technology is that it generally winds up saving you lots of time that you can put to better and more profitable use elsewhere.

❖ Take a techie out to lunch. Seriously, if you've got somebody in your office who's good at all that, make alliances. Maybe you've got expertise in something that you can offer in return.

❖ I'm very good at technology, but others I know who are also good in that area are pretty bad when it comes to people skills. If you're a "techie," I think you need to ask yourself some questions. Are you patient when explaining things to other people? Do you use technology as a way to build a wall around you? Do you speak in a language that non-technologically oriented people cannot understand?

Case Management Systems

Working with case management software can be one of the most significant ways that a paralegal interfaces with technology.

❖ Our experience with our case management system taught us a valuable lesson: everyone had to get behind it. In the beginning, we had a lot of grousing about it but now the expectation is that if you're in this firm, than you need to have a basic level of computer literacy so that you can utilize this system. That's just the way it is.

❖ I have friends whose supervising attorneys won't or can't be bothered with CMS. That's a bunch of malarkey. Successful use of CMS requires a genuine "top-down" mentality.

❖ I work in a practice that has just a few partners and I have to say that I come from a very different kind of background than they do. My parents owned a farm supply store, and from an early age I was helping with the books. I got a sense of how a business runs, how you compare your current year with your last year and the year before that, and how you project into the year ahead. Our partners are not really business people, but a law firm does need to be run as a business and when I realized that CMS could do that for us, I brought it to the attention of the powers that be. Now we use CMS to tell us where our cases are coming from, how many we get through advertising and what the return rate is like on our ad expenses, what kinds of cases are generating the most income for the firm, and so on. Everybody's really excited about it and, if I can blow my own horn for a minute, I'm the one who made it happen!

❖ No law firm should expect that when you introduce CMS, you do it for the whole firm overnight. People would go into shock! You have to introduce it slowly, with measurable goals, like one department at a time, let's say. The point of this is not to drive people away, but, rather, to make their lives easier.

❖ Your CMS is as good as the training provided. Make sure that the training being offered is absolutely top-notch.

E-mail

Even if you're technophobic, chances are you've made your peace with, and have even come to love, e-mail. Aside from the junk that so regularly comes down the pipe, why wouldn't you? E-mail is easy, it's fast, it's fun, it saves scads of time, and it makes distant corners of the world feel nearby. Still, there are "good" e-mailers and "not-so-good" e-mailers. Which one are you?

❖ Never *ever* send junk! If you're not sure whether something is junk or not, it probably is and that means don't send it. The two main things I hate to see coming in are jokes and hoaxes. Ninety-nine percent of the humor that people send me is about as funny as watching a fat man fall off a bicycle. Even worse are those horrible public safety messages, about some new kind of malady that you can get from eating a Moon Pie while standing on your head or whatever, and then, by the next day, the sender's bothering you with an apology because he found out it wasn't true. If you receive an e-mail that has something so scary in it that you think you ought to send it on to your friends and loved ones, check first with http://www.urbanlegends.com. They keep track of hoaxes and will let you know if what you're sending on is real or a potential embarrassment for you.

❖ I never open attachments from anyone I don't know. That's a very likely way to welcome in a virus.

❖ Don't ever write your e-mail in all caps. It's so hard to read.

❖ There are real confidentiality issues around e-mail. For instance, a client may give you his e-mail address at work and may encourage you to communicate with him via e-mail. But if you are going to be sending him information of a personal matter, let's say around his divorce proceedings, you have to make sure that he understands that this information could conceivably be seen by other eyes.

❖ I print hard copies of all my e-mails to and from clients and I put them in their files. Better safe than sorry.

❖ Some people regard e-mail as an excuse for highly casual, even sloppy writing. I don't. I still use a salutation such as I would use in a letter—"Dear Mr. Jones," let's say—and I still pay attention to the content, the grammar, the punctuation, the spelling, and all those old-fashioned things.

❖ E-mail is not the place for any special formatting, because your recipient may be on another system and it will all be for naught. That means no underlining, no bolds, no italics, no indentatations. Separate paragraphs by double-spacing. Keep it easy and simple—that's the joy of it.

❖ Your subject line is important, particularly if you're sending an e-mail to someone who receives dozens a day. You want yours to stick out, but without revealing anything confidential. A word like URGENT in the subject line can be effective.

❖ Signal confidentiality in your e-mail. You can use the confidentiality statement you use on your fax cover sheets, or you can just put the word CONFIDENTIAL at the top of the message.

❖ One danger of e-mail is that it tends to make all people into writers. And some things are better left unwritten, just as they are left unsaid. I know people who have had conflicts with their co-workers and then run back to their desks and send off an e-mail tirade to them. This is a terrible thing to do, even worse than having it out face-to-face, because, once written, these missives are here for posterity and may well come back to haunt you.

❖ Always think a moment before you push SEND. Do you really want to send that e-mail? Once you do, you can never UNSEND it!

WAR STORIES: HAVE WE MET?

We have one attorney in my office who forgets which paralegal he assigns projects to or what work he has requested to be done on projects. I do two things to deal with this: first, I create a list of all of the current cases along with a column for assigned paralegal, status, deadlines, and when completed. We keep this list current by working with the attorney's secretary. Second, I prepare a form titled "Paralegal Notes." This document is filled out by the paralegal working on a case and is placed in the "attorney's notes and memos" folder for any work performed on a case, phone calls, or whatever is needed.

CHAPTER 8

Life in the Litigation Lane

In this chapter, we will be looking at some of the special concerns of paralegals working in the area of litigation, one of the more important avenues of employment in the field. Litigation paralegals will most likely be doing extensive legal research, including shepherding cases and writing briefs. The litigation paralegal might also have to explore legislative history and draft preliminary answers to written interrogatories or draft preliminary interrogatories for the opposing attorney. A litigation paralegal may, as well, be involved in maintaining an office "tickler" system, the supervising attorney's calendar, client files, and more.

GENERAL REFLECTIONS

❖ I love this area of law because I get to dig to my heart's content. I must have been a badger in another life. I relish the responsibility of having to search for the facts that make or break a case. It feels important to me.

❖ I think litigation is a great area, because intellectually it may be the most stimulating for a paralegal. The big challenge is finding an attorney you can enjoy working with. In my experience, too many of them have to be prodded to stay on task and on schedule, and then there are those who are raging bulls, waiting to be tamed. Sometimes it feels like the middle ground is definitely underpopulated.

❖ The best overall advice I could give to a paralegal entering into the area of litigation is to get a well-rounded education in all areas of law, because litigation touches on everything.

❖ Litigation is not an area of law where you can afford to slip up. The consequences can be severe. So ask questions. All the time. There are no dumb questions. Just check in with your attorney a lot.

❖ I started out in the work world as a reporter on a small-town newspaper. I loved it, but you've got to make a living, right? Well, being a litigation paralegal pays me a living wage but it also feeds my interest in investigation. I don't know—maybe I read too many *Nancy Drew* books when I was young—but finding the facts is still my idea of fun.

❖ For me, it's all about the courtroom. For an actor, it's about going out on stage, or if you're a trapeze artist it's about being in the center ring with the sawdust and the bright lights. Well, I get that kind of charge from walking into a courtroom. It's that combination of something that's very structured and formalized but that still has this extraordinary element of surprise. You never really know what's going to happen, particularly when a jury is involved.

❖ I really enjoy working with my friends in the medical offices. I love learning about medical matters. Maybe I should have been a doctor or a nurse!

❖ One skill that I draw upon as a litigation paralegal is an artistic talent that I definitely had as a child but that got lost somewhere along the way (probably because my parents didn't put any stock in artistic accomplishments). I'm very good at helping to create trial exhibits and charts and so forth. I get a lot of pleasure out of that.

❖ I work for a very brilliant attorney. I could never think on all the levels that she manages to operate on; the fact that I can offer support for her, and help organize her and be part of her team, is something I'm very proud of.

❖ I enjoy the ongoing educational experience of being a litigation paralegal. And, believe me, you've got to take that ongoing education seriously because the law changes every year. State legislatures are always passing new statutes and rules and you have to stay abreast of them. One way to be considered valuable in your firm is to take on the task of keeping track of these changes, sending around a memo periodically. I always check legal periodicals right after the first of the year to find out what's new.

❖ To me, what distinguishes a good paralegal from a *really* good paralegal is that the latter has read the code books. Now I understand that reading code books is not everyone's idea of a swell time, but it's really, really important. Paralegals should not be overly reliant on their supervising attorneys for this kind of knowledge. You need to take the time to learn for yourself things like discovery rules or rules for motions or briefs, or judgments or liens.

QUICK TIPS FOR LITIGATION PARALEGALS

Here is a whole bunch of time-savers. On your mark, get set, go!

Calendaring

❖ Get to the mail first! Whenever mail winds up on my attorney's desk before mine, a scary thing happens—it disappears. So I make sure that I get to the mail first and, before that mail gets routed, the dates go down on my calendar.

❖ I like to leave behind a trail, to show that I did the work I was supposed to do, in case anyone ever doubts me,. So whenever I go through papers and see dates that need to be calendared, I use a highlighter to mark a "C" over the top of the date. Highlighters, as you probably know, don't show up on photocopies, so the document is not compromised in any way. I use the same system on outgoing documents. Once we've sent a deposition, I'll highlight a "C" over the date on the deposition notice.

❖ Whenever I send out a notice that is in any way time-sensitive, I'll make a note of it on my copy. For instance, if I've sent a form to a government agency and need a response back by 4/15/2003, let's say, I'll mark with highlighter on the copy "4/15/2003." That'll be a flag to me if my attorney asks if we've gotten such-and-such back, and I'll just open the file and I'll see the yellow highlighter staring up at me with the anticipated response date.

❖ We've usually got a crazy deposition schedule in our office, so here's the system I use. I keep an individual physical file on each of our clients just for their deposition history, with all the specifics I need to keep track, including the date, time, and location of the deposition. These files contain copies of Notices of Deposition, subpoenas, and certified mail receipts as well. Then I like to keep a running master file of all our depositions that are pending, again with time, place, and locations of the depositions, so I can juggle dates at a glance, as I need to. I keep another calendar of depositions on my desk calendar, in case I'm on the phone and I can't even find a second to reach for something.

File Management

❖ When you're a litigation paralegal, you'd better get used to being part of a team, because that's the name of the game. And you're likely to have quite a few players on that team, from any assortment of partners to associate attorneys, other legal assistants, secretaries, and, who knows, maybe even a nurse-paralegal thrown into the mix. As a result, the file in question may get spread out rather thin, and when you're tackling an assignment, you might not find what you need. For this reason, you may want to consider creating some kind of working file or quick-look list of components that are related to the case. Of course, you'll start with the client's name, the case title, and file number, and then you'll want to create some kind of ledger or set of columns upon which to record the essential information. This includes the date that the file is opened, the date the client's records are received, a list of people who have used the file, contact information for insurance company officials, and so on.

❖ The key organizing step for me when I create a file is to create, at the same time, a contact list which I insert on the inside front cover of the file. I keep a copy in a separate notebook. Among the items I've got on my contact list are the names, snail mail addresses, e-mail addresses, phone numbers and fax numbers of the client, the opposing counsel, the opposing parties if opposing counsel is not involved, the name and address of the court where the case is venued, and the case number. Now obviously you can customize your contact sheet with anybody else you think might be useful, like the names and numbers of the opposing counsel's secretary and/or assistants, the court reporter, the judge's staff, a good takeout deli in the vicinity of the court, and so on. The contact list is a work in progress, and should reflect any changes in the cast of players.

❖ I've worked in different offices with different filing systems and the only ones that I thought had any kind of clarity to their process were the ones where there were separate folders for each type of discovery. I know of offices that have separate folders for every single set of discovery propounded and its response.

❖ Documents mustn't be removed from a client file or subfile. The documents should only be moved with the whole file. That way you can keep track of your documents.

❖ I have a really good filing system and when people ask me what my secret is, I tell them it's not so much secrets as it is a few guiding principles. First of all, filing systems need to be scrupulously planned out and it's unlikely you're going to buy the kind of time you need for that in the course of a busy work week. That means you may have to give over a weekend of two to come in and get the job done to your satisfaction. Another guiding principle to keep in mind is that the system has to be clear enough and simple enough for everyone to understand it. You're not going to be the only one using it. Secretaries, file clerks, and receptionists all need access to the files and if you're not there, you don't want to put them in the position where they have to get a code breaker to come in and figure things out.

❖ Think labels. Labels, labels, labels. Can't get enough of 'em.

❖ Don't stint on the subfiles. Create as many as you need. The more subfiles you use, the better organized you'll be.

❖ It's critical that your filing system observes all the rules of client confidentiality. You may want to use numeric labeling or some other form of encryption to assure that.

❖ Closing files is a whole other important area. You need to follow state and national standards regarding file retention, and you'll have to develop a procedure for destroying files, which usually means shredding.

❖ I've put together The Big Book on court procedure. My book tells me which courts permit filing of documents by fax, for instance, and which courts require that the attorney has to appear in person at motion hearings.

There are a lot of little peculiarities among the courts, from one to the other, and The Big Book's got them all down.

❖ If a case is extremely complex, consider outsourcing the document tracking. Specialists in this field will do a whole lot better job than you ever could.

Outsourcing

❖ When we're pressed for time, we use a summary service for our deposition transcripts. If you go that route, just make sure you're shopping comparatively so that you can get the best service for the best price.

❖ Never feel that, if you're under the gun time-wise, you have to be loyal to one provider. Your first order of loyalty is to your firm and to your client, to get the best job done, so if you have to use two different summary services at the same time, let's say, to meet your deadlines, don't worry about it.

❖ I work in a region where services like summary services are rare, if nonexistent. But with the Internet, you can find what you need anywhere, ship it out overnight mail, get it back overnight mail, and it's not a whole lot different than if you had such a service in an industrial park down the road, So when it comes to making your life easier, don't be limited by geography.

❖ My rule of thumb is that if a case involves more than ten boxes of documents, I call in a document control company to take car of things. Given the luxury of having your documents scanned, coded, and copied onto floppys or CDs, the price is really not so forbidding.

❖ I've taken it upon myself to act as a kind of Zagat within the firm, maintaining a list of vendors, agencies, attorneys in other cities, and so on. I make thumbnail notes about the type of service they offer and the quality of their work. Just by letting my fingers do the walking, I can go through my file and come up with a crackerjack court reporter in Cincinnati or a proficient process server in Peoria. I've also got printing services; rental car agencies; air shuttle buses; travel agents; delivery and messenger servises, hotels, investigators, mediators, caterer's . . . you name it. I even have a rating system of one to four stars. What a feeling of power it gives me!

Telephone Tips

❖ Fast and furious is the name of the game in many litigation practices. The phone is ringing constantly and you can't afford to mess up messages. So the first rule is to always get the name of the person you spoke with. Sometime the conversation seems completely unmemorable and you can't imagine why you should bother making note of it, but you'd be surprised. Even little innocuous conversations can wind up playing a big role in terms of the evidence chain.

❖ To me, being a litigation paralegal without a phone log sheet is like being an astronaut without a space suit. Do you honestly think you can keep track of little pieces of paper without slipping up somewhere along the line? Come on! The phone log will also act like a kind of diary for you, so when your attorney asks you six months later "if we ever sent yadda-yadda to yadda-yadda," you'll be able to find the proof.

The Client Interview

As a paralegal, you may often find yourself in the position of being first in your firm to encounter a potential new client. Here's the drill:

❖ I screen a lot of new clients, or potential clients, because it's cost-productive to have me do so. Many of the people who contact us are not desirable to take on as clients, and my time is cheaper than my attorney's.

❖ If you're screening potential clients, you'd better have a good grip on who does what in your firm. You should know that Attorney X does family law and Attorney Y does securities, or whatever. Have a fix too on what these attorneys' respective billing rates are. Keep in mind, after all, that a lot of people will find attorneys out of the phone book and your prices just may not gibe with their pocketbooks.

❖ If you're going to be referring people to attorneys outside of the firm, assuming that their problems don't mesh with your specialties (or your price are too rich for their blood), then make sure that your referral list is current. Check in with your attorney periodically to determine if the names on the referral list are as they should be.

❖ Different practices have very different procedures and standards when it comes to paralegals screening potential clients. Just make sure you're working with a supervising attorney to guard against any UPL issues when you're doing the screening. Always keep in the forefront of your consciousness the rule that you cannot counsel or give legal advice to a potential client, even if your firm does not undertake representation. That cannot be stated too strongly. On the other hand, your supervising attorney may tell you that it's okay for you to suggest to a potential client that he or she take the matter to a small claims court, for instance.

❖ First order of business when taking a call from a potential client is to identify yourself and to make it clear that you are a legal assistant or paralegal and not a lawyer.

❖ I've made a form for myself that I fill out whenever I have a telephone conversation with a prospective client. I like the form because it reminds me to ask every question I need to ask.

❖ Whenever I've screened a potential client, I'll immediately e-mail around to all the attorneys and other paralegals in the office to determine whether anyone is aware of any reason why we should not take on this person as a client.

❖ I've found that 90 percent of all potential clients will ask me, "How much is this going to cost?" There's only one suitable answer to that: "I don't know. You will have to speak with Attorney X."

❖ I worked in a firm once where one of our paralegals was very haughty. She acted like she was the maitre d' in a fancy French restaurant, and was quite peremptory with potential clients whom she felt were not going to translate into big fees. Well, one of the people she blew off was an out-of-work schoolteacher who went on to start a software firm and become a zillionaire. If she had acted toward him in the kind of courteous and friendly way that all paralegals should act toward all potential clients, maybe he would have remembered the firm when it was time for him to start making lawyers rich.

Evidence
Keeping track of evidence can be an important part of a paralegal's job.

❖ This is pretty elemental, but your evidence log should always start with a form upon which you enter the file name, a description of the evidence, and notes about how the evidence was acquired, as in who handed it over and when. You'll also want to include any identifying marks, the name of the evidence custodian, and other such relevant information.

❖ The thrust of the evidence log is to show the chain of custody that the evidence has passed through. That means a column of names, dates, and the reason why the evidence passed into the hands of any given person.

❖ Your evidence log should include a statement that says that the evidence must be protected and that it must be returned in the condition in which it was lent out. Whoever asks to remove the evidence has to sign this statement.

❖ For extra security, I take a snapshot of the evidence, recording what it looked like, before and after each release.

Interrogatories

Interrogatories are among the most important forms used by litigation paralegals. Develop your skill at crafting effective ones.

❖ Before you ever sit down to write interrogatories, you need to have a clear sense of their scope and their limits. The questions have to be relevant to the matter at hand, and, in fact, the judge may well limit them. Interrogatories are not there to overwhelm an opposing attorney with paperwork. That is highly unethical. Consider your questions, because poorly crafted questions result in objections, and objections result in loss of time and possibly valuable information. Are any of your interrogatories vague? Irrelevant? Do you have too many of them and do they cover too long a period of time? Do they probe into areas of privileged information? Test them out on yourself before sending them along to anyone else (including your supervising attorney, who's not going to want to have to correct your work).

❖ I like to plot out a rough outline for my interrogatories that's built around three questions: What do I have? What do I have that's not quite good enough yet? And what do I need to get?

❖ As with almost everything else in law, don't try to reinvent the wheel every time. Amass a master set of interrogatories that can be adapted for your needs as they come up.

❖ I like to approach my interrogatories like I'm a reporter, with the famous "Who, what, where, when, why, and how" questions. I keep the pleadings right up front, and then I craft my interrogatories to support or rebut the allegations made in the pleadings.

❖ Keep it simple. Keep your sentences short, neat, and clean. No misspellings!

❖ What's the difference between Barbara Walters and a bad interviewer? A bad interviewer asks questions that can be answered by "yes" or "no." You should be a Barbara Walters. Make your questions targeted and hard to slip in and out of.

❖ I always try to include a sort of global question for the end that covers anything I may have left out. Something like, "Tell us any information pertinent to this suit that has not been set out in your previous answers." These kinds of questions may not always be that effective, but sometimes they are, and sometimes is good enough for me.

❖ Don't waste your time. Before you draft your interrogatories, always check with the court in which the action is being filed to see if there are limits to the number of interrogatories that you can submit.

❖ I always have my supervising attorney go over my interrogatories and my responses to interrogatories. I never try to go it alone. Why should I? That's what he's there for.

Depositions

Depositions are like interrogatories, but are usually conducted orally and have their own set of guidelines.

❖ As paralegals, our job is to summarize the depositions. Your first question is going to be: How am I supposed to summarize this? Sometimes it's chronologically; sometimes it's by the legal issue or the factual issue or perhaps some other organizing principle. You need to get the thumbs-up from your attorney in this regard and then you can go to work.

❖ Reading and highlighting, reading and highlighting . . . that's what it's all about. I change the color of my highlighter every so often so I don't get bored.

❖ Maybe this goes without saying, but always include the page number and line number when you're making a point in your summary.

❖ At this point in the 21st century, you should be using some good summarizing software. If you're not, I honestly don't understand why.

❖ When it comes to indexing your deposition transcripts, you'd be amazed at some of the services that court reporters are offering these days for really nominal sums. To get an overview of what's out there and how it works, check out the website of the National Court Reporters Association at http://www.verbatimreporters.com.

Expert Witnesses

As a litigation paralegal, you may have responsibility for locating and working with expert witnesses.

❖ Most sourcing of expert witnesses, particularly within the medical realm, is done by referrals and word-of-mouth. Somebody in your firm has used somebody successfully, or your contacts in another firm can recommend someone. With more unusual circumstances, like a rare medical condition, for instance, you may have to do some legwork. Generally, that means networking with the pool of medical witnesses you've already amassed.

❖ This may date me, but I remember the pre-Internet era and to have a resource like the Internet when you're looking for expert witnesses is like landing a man on the moon! Seriously, you can type in any keyword on a good search engine, and it can be something as arcane as Zulu Medicine Man, and, nine times out of ten, something will come up. Some kind of lead. Maybe you'll be directed to a book on amazon.com or something but that will be a start.

❖ A fertile area when searching for expert witnesses are trade publications and trade organizations. Every industry—and I do mean *every* industry—has them. And, boy, are they willing to help you round up work for their members.

❖ When you're stumped, and if you're willing to shell out some money, you can use a search firm to find an expert for your particular need. Technical Advisory Service for Attorneys (http://www.tasanet.com) and Association of Scientific Advisors (http://www.asaexperts.com) are two such resources, but there are plenty more. You might want to try Expert Witnesses Online (http://www.online-expert.net) or American Medical Forensic Specialists (http://www.amfs.com), to name two more.

❖ I've made up a directory of expert witnesses. It contains their résumés and any other relevant material, like articles about them, for instance, and I update it regularly. Sort of my very own "Who's Who" of expert witnesses.

❖ The first order of business after you've located and contacted an expert is to make sure there are no conflict of interest issues. Then ask for a complete résumé. Also, rough out a schedule to make sure that an expert will be able to be on hand at the time of the court date. If not, go on to the next expert.

❖ If you're chosen to have the first meeting with the expert—and my supervising attorney often asks me to do exactly that—then you need to be prepared with a good list of questions. First off is the conflict-of-interest issue. Then you might want to know if the expert's worked on this kind of subject matter before. Did he or she work on the side of the plaintiff or the defendant? How many trials has the expert testified in? What were the outcomes of those trials? Don't be shy. You're paying!

❖ When you're meeting with the expert, not only do you have to ask the right questions but also you have to keep your eyes and ears open and let your first impressions guide you. Is the expert neatly dressed or does he have a large spaghetti sauce stain on his tie? Does she mumble? Does he carry on in double-talk or is she a *grande dame* who'll alienate the "common people" of the jury? Does he have shifty eyes and a five o'clock shadow at nine o'clock in the morning?

❖ I don't put any store in videotaped expert testimony. I don't think juries do either.

❖ If you've got the budget for it, try running your expert's name through the jury verdict and settlement libraries of Lexis-Nexis or Westlaw and see what comes up. You may get a pretty good overview of how many trials the expert's been involved in and how he or she has done.

❖ Never give an expert a document or information that you don't want the opposing side to see. All the work you do with the expert is discoverable.

❖ Experts can really blow your budget. Choreograph their appearances so they're not standing around on your coin.

❖ One thing I want to say about experts: they often act like experts. In other words, they can be real prima donnas. We've all heard horror stories about putting up experts in hotels and having them order Dom Perignon and Beluga caviar from room service. It's a dicey business working with experts, so watch your step . . . and theirs!

Exhibits and Other Trial Support

❖ Sometimes I'll watch some lawyer show on TV and I'll marvel at the kind of exhibits they get together for a trial. Unfortunately, I do not work for Johnnie Cochran and our exhibits budget is circumscribed. If you can relate to what I'm saying, I'm wondering if you've heard of the DQ2 bank. It's a kind of litigation graphics catalog, with over 2,000 generic exhibits. You'll find charts, maps, medical illustrations. Check it out at www.decisionquest.com

❖ When you're in the grip of a trial, with all that intensity, exhibits have a way of stacking up very quickly. What I do to exercise some control over all that is to make individual tabbed file folders marked "Exhibit 1," "Exhibit 2," and so on. This allows me to put my hands on any exhibit at a moment's notice when we're in the heat of the trial. And, of course, once you've filed the exhibits away after the trial, you can reuse these temporary files for your next trial.

❖ Creating trial videos is something that I've often found myself involved in as a paralegal. It can be a slippery slope, as some of the vendors are not so great. Always use someone highly recommended and preview that person's work. Arrange to meet the vendor at the location where the videotape will be made, so you can compare notes. Above all else, make sure that the final product is realistic. You do not want your courtroom video to look like *Magnum P.I.* or whatever. And make sure the video is in reasonable shape before passing it along to the attorney. You don't want to be embarrassed by passing along a bad product.

FUTURE PLANNING FOR LITIGATION PARALEGALS

The litigation area, if it's right for you, can be a genuinely exciting arena. But what if things are not moving at the rate you hoped they would? What if you've been working in a practice for a couple of years and you'd like to raise the career stakes a little? Here are a few ideas from those who have been in that position:

- ❖ Start with your supervising attorney. Have a heart-to-heart—*at a time when it is convenient to your attorney*—and let it be known that you feel you can do more and you'd like to do more. What kind of new responsibilities can you take on?

- ❖ Network with other paralegals in the firm and see how you and they can support each other. Maybe you know something they'd like to learn and vice versa. United we stand!

- ❖ Be bold. Approach an attorney in another area of the firm that interests you and let him or her know it. Maybe you're in litigation but you'd rather be in trusts and estates. Don't be shy. Asking is not going to get you into any trouble. If you're good, the firm is not going to want to lose you and will want to make sure you're happy.

- ❖ Diversify within the firm by using some of your spare time to work in other areas where you can get to know other players. For instance, you might want to volunteer to work on a pro bono project. Maybe you're great with food or decorations and you want to help out with the firm's big summer picnic. It never hurts to get yourself around.

WAR STORIES:
HOME AGAIN, HOME AGAIN, JIGGETY JIG . . .

My supervising attorney has an unusual habit: he likes to just go home when he wants. He's a partner in the firm, but will often just disappear for the day around 2 P.M.! It can be kind of embarrassing when clients call, expecting him back after lunch, and he doesn't come back after lunch. I used to feel like I had to make excuses for him, but I don't really enjoy making up stories, so I just stopped. Instead, I'd just take the message, and that was it.

I haven't figured out how to stop him from leaving for the day—he's a free spirit; there's no stopping him—but he does check his voice mail regularly so at least I can get a message to him.

Some time I'd like to just leave at two in the afternoon, and see how he'd like it. Maybe he'd think it was a great idea!

CHAPTER 9

The Corporate Culture and Other Paralegal Venues

The corporate world offers enormous opportunities for the paralegal. In this chapter, we will look at some of the special circumstances of working within corporate legal departments. Of course,
not everyone's experience is the same, so you will have to judge
which of these reflections sound on-target to you. We will then have
a whirlwind "tips tour" through some of the other areas in which
paralegals work.

GOING CORPORATE

Quite a few paralegals opt to leave areas of law like litigation for jobs
in the corporate world. Let us hear what they have to say.

❖ Generally the money's better and the hours are better.
The money's better, the hours are better, and the people
are saner. Should I keep going?

❖ When you work in the corporate world, you come out
from under the thumb of billable hours. Some people
thrive on billable hours. They have an entrepreneurial
streak and the necessity to push themselves feeds that
streak. Others like the security and relative calm of the
corporate world, where you get paid the same amount
no matter how much work you generate. It took me a
while to figure out which of these orientations I was
more comfortable with, but now I know. I really didn't
want to live my life in such a way that if my teenage

daughter calls me up to ask which of two pairs of shoes she should buy, I have to worry about spending ten minutes on the phone with her that isn't going toward my billable hours.

❖ Do you really want to know why I made the switch from litigation to corporate? Because I was getting colitis from all the pressure in litigation, that's why.

❖ Look, some people go into law because they grew up on *L.A. Law* or *Law and Order* or whatever and they want that kind of drama in their lives. Litigation can give you that. Other people, like myself, went into this field because they wanted a nice, clean job that paid well. I like the corporate world. I don't want to be surrounded by people with rolled-up shirt sleeves and pencils behind their ears, sweating bullets that if the decision doesn't come down in their favor they won't be able to pay that month's rent bill. I like working in a beautiful corporate headquarters, with a gorgeous glassed-in commissary that overlooks a pond with swans. Call me shallow, but it makes me happy.

❖ I really enjoy the nuts-and-bolts, day-to-day activities of the corporate world. It's funny—sometimes I feel like corporations are this enormous zoo animal, like a hippo or an elephant, in danger of extinction even, and I'm like the trainer. I take care to make sure that its needs are met. I schedule meetings; I draft the agendas and the minutes; I prepare and review contracts. I do all kinds of things to help keep this big lumbering animal alive and I've really grown to become quite fond of it.

❖ There's a lot of good research to be done in the corporate world. People sometimes think that the secretarial aspect of being a legal assistant is accentuated in the corporate world, but I find plenty of intellectual stimulation in researching the laws and regulations that affect our corporation.

❖ Why do I prefer working in the corporate world to working in a law practice? Easy. In a law practice, there's a ceiling. I'm never going to ascend to the level of the attorneys. In a corporation, however, if I prove myself to be a capable and even outstanding paralegal, I could very well work my way into a management position. That wouldn't be so bad for a little girl from South Philly!

❖ I found it to be a big adjustment going from a law firm to a corporate job. At first, I felt like I had died and gone to heaven. I could go downstairs, get myself a latté, call a friend and find out what she was doing Saturday night. This was how people were meant to live! But then I started to get nervous. In my law firm job, I never had an empty desk. There was always work to do, lots of it. But here there were days when I had virtually nothing to do. In time, I came to realize that the nature of my work was that I had a lot of long-term projects, things that weren't due for two weeks or more. I had to structure my own time and make sure I was working productively. It felt weird.

❖ I think some people go into the corporate sector thinking that they're going to be on easy street after the stress of working in a litigation practice, but it isn't so. The corporation today, with the economy the way it is and the move toward mergers and conglomeration, is just as intense as any litigation practice. You not only have to handle corporation filings, but you need to be thoroughly versed in checking state and federal trademark filings and name availability. Then you have to deal with preparing bylaws and regulations. You'll need to maintain the corporate minute book. You're liable to have a ton of document drafting to do. You may have to interface with the IRS or other government agencies. You should never assume that when you get a corporate job, that means you get to put your feet up on your desk and polish your toenails.

❖ When I took a job in corporate, I felt like I was thrown into the deep end of the pool without my water wings. Not that I didn't know how to do the work, but we didn't have any in-house counsel. I was interfacing with outside counsel, and that meant that on the inside, it was I who was making all the decisions. At first, it was scary, but now I'm used to people asking me for my opinion.

❖ It can be a challenge to figure out what you're worth to a corporation and then to try to get it. In a law firm, the billable hours make it easy to figure out your worth. It's basically a kind of simple equation. But that isn't true of a corporation. Corporations don't make money off paralegals; paralegals are there the way the computers are there or the furniture or the air conditioning system. We are necessary, but we are regarded, more or less, as an asset and our compensation is regarded as overhead. We don't actually make the candy bars or nylon stockings or crayons that the corporation turns out to keep afloat. So when you go to ask for a raise, you have to figure out why you really deserve one and that can be intimidating.

❖ When I started in corporate ten years ago, it was a different world. It felt expansive and powerful. Now when I tell people I work in a large corporation in the legal department, they look at me like maybe I'm the one cooking the books.

❖ It's been my experience in moving from a law office to corporate that I have to work really hard to get people in the corporation to trust me. I think there is a lot of paranoia floating around these big corporations today—there probably always was—and if there is anything that tends to set off paranoid thinking, it's a lawyer. I may not be a lawyer, but in the eyes of my colleagues, I'm the next closest thing.

❖ If you're going to work in corporate, you've got to like sports metaphors. You're always hearing about how you have to be a team player and all that stuff. Well, I made up my mind to be a team player *extraordinaire.* When I worked in law practices, I pretty much went my own way, but here, if I want to get ahead, I have to cultivate people in a more socially-interactive way, not just rely on the quality of my work. My supervisor's favorite charity is juvenile diabetes so who do you think is out there doing the Walkathon with her? Little old team player me!

❖ Look, let's call a spade a spade. Lawyers in their own practice, for the most part—at least the ones I've worked in—are of an entrepreneurial bent. Corporations, on the other hand, are absolutely replete with bureaucracy. Heaven forbid you should look at somebody the wrong way—they'll get Human Resources after you in a second. Taking the day off for your kid's first day in school can be an exercise in navigating red tape. But, hey, nothing's perfect, and I still value the fact that I don't have to meet that billable quota month after month.

❖ It's a world of difference between a law office and a corporation, like day and night. And you can tell just how

EMPLOYMENT POLICIES

The first thing to do when you arrive in your new job (and this can include any job, not just one in the corporate world) is to request a look at the employment policy handbook. Pay careful attention to the policies regarding the following:

- Vacation time (in your first, second, and third years and beyond)
- Holidays observed
- Amount of sick leave allowed
- When you are expected to arrive at the workplace
- Grounds for termination

In addition to your personal stake in reviewing these policies, you may find that, as a paralegal, your department has the responsibility for continually reviewing and updating these handbooks.

different they are simply by going for a job in corporate. You won't even meet an attorney until your second or third interview. First you've got to run the gauntlet past the Human Resources people. Oh, and don't forget that you'll be asked to fill out a job application. This can be a bit of a shock if you haven't had to do this when getting a position in a law practice. So come prepared with your license, phone numbers of references, addresses, and all the rest.

❖ I couldn't make head or tails of the job titles when I first went into corporate. Contract Administrator? Labor Relations Specialist? Technical Information Specialist? Human Resources Staff Analyst? What language were we talking?

❖ Why do I choose corporate? The perks. Great health plan, 401(k)s, a health club membership, even dry cleaning! And, whereas I used to sit in a cubicle at my law firm, here I have a private office. That means a lot to me.

❖ I had to make a choice. I loved my work in the law firm where I'd been for quite some time, but when I got pregnant, I got an offer from a corporation where they had on-site day care. It was an offer I couldn't refuse.

❖ One of the really important issues in the life of a paralegal is continuing education. When your education stops, you more or less stop, if you know what I mean. One of the things I love about my corporate job is that the educational opportunities are so good and so easy to partake of. I get 40 hours of in-house educational seminars and computerized classes a year. On top of that, I get tuition and textbook reimbursement for any courses I take at an accredited college. Now is there any law firm you know of, outside of the blue chip ones in New York, L.A., and Chicago, which can match that?

❖ I went into this field because I love the law. And I still love it. But, having transferred over to the corporate world, I realize how much I love money too. Sorry to say so, but it's the truth. And in the corporate world, the money adds up, when you take into account the matching employer contributions to my retirement account and the employee stock purchase program I can take advantage of.

❖ There are a lot of benefits to working in the corporate world, and, of course, some drawbacks. One of the benefits that I think gets the least attention is the independence that you can have in the corporate setting. This almost sounds paradoxical, because you would think that the hierarchical structure of the corporation would produce the opposite of independence. But the fact is that law firms to me seem even more hierarchical, in the sense that paralegals are never going to get onto a level playing field with attorneys. In a corporate setting, paralegals rarely have outside clients so the supervision issue is not as pressing. You still have to keep UPL in mind, but in the corporate setting you may actually find yourself without an attorney to report to. In fact, you may be the only legal person in the whole place!

❖ A word of warning: some people go into the corporate world thinking they're going to be making so much more money than they would have if they worked in a law firm. The fact is, however, that in a law firm, if you're good, it's up to a few people who have all the decision-making authority to authorize raises how and when they see fit. In a corporation, your raise may be determined by what others around you are making and you may find it a long haul to work your way up the pay scales. The money in the corporate world is often more about the benefits than the salary.

❖ It's really key, if you're going to thrive as a corporate paralegal, to network with other corporate paralegals. You may have dealings, for instance, in other states. Well, you're going to need help with that and how are you going to get it? I start by looking in Martindale-Hubbell for legal departments in corporations in the geographic area where I have dealings, and I pick up the phone and make a connection. I explain the situation and, nine times out of ten, that paralegal from Idaho or Iowa or New Mexico will fax me the forms I need. And, nine times out of ten, I'll hear back from that person somewhere down the line, and I'll return the favor. That's the beauty of it.

❖ If you feel like you can't do the legwork and meet your deadlines in time when doing out-of-state filings, check into a corporate service company. You'll be able to locate many of these if you type in the term as a keyword on any Internet search engine, or you can network with other corporate paralegals to find out who they use.

QUICK TIPS FOR CORPORATE PARALEGALS

Make your life easier with the following time-saving tips.

Minute Books

The maintenance of corporate minute books is a large part of most corporate paralegal jobs. Here are some thoughts on the topic.

❖ Minute books aren't optional. Whatever kind of corporation you are in—for-profit, not-for-profit, limited liability, partnership, limited partnership—you'll need a place for the company records. The minute book, which is also called the company records book or just the record book, is that place.

❖ The book should look like this: there should be an index of sections, with each section separated by written or numbered tabs. Within those sections, documents are to be filed in chronological order. The section tabs should include Certificates of Articles of Incorporation; bylaws and amendments; stockholder minutes; incorporator minutes; directors' minutes; foreign qualification filings; IRS filings; stock ledger and certificates; and maybe copies of annual reports.

❖ It's important to have a summary sheet as part of the minute book. That's the place where you get your quick, at-a-glance reference to the corporate name; the state and date of incorporation; the purpose of the business; the names of directors and names and titles of officers; the end of the fiscal year; and other such items you want to get to fast when you need them. Just make sure that this information is always updated and fully accurate.

❖ Like everything else in the world, minute book maintenance has entered into a whole new era with the advent of advanced technology. Check out a software program called Corporate Focus from Two Step Software, Inc. (http://www.twostep.com) that can electronically maintain minute books and stock records. It's a huge help.

Reviewing Corporate Policies

It is common for the review of corporate policies and procedures to come under the jurisdiction of the corporate paralegal. Listen to how some of your colleagues approach this task:

❖ The policies have to be airtight. In fact, it helps to assess a policy by approaching it as if you were a 25-year-veteran of the corporation who's just been fired by some young whippersnapper. Every fiber of your body wants to sue! As the paralegal reviewing these policies, you have to find where you're vulnerable to disgruntled and litigious employees.

❖ All policies have a sign-off section, or an approval section, in which the right person signs on the right dotted line to make the whole thing kosher. You'll have to pay careful attention to this approval section to make sure that the signature line has a typed name and title under it, for instance. Only a department head or a manager should sign off on these, by the way.

❖ The policy will most likely have a definitions section, or at least they should. The purpose of this section is so that people can understand what it's all about. So what's the point of a policy if you need the input of a translator with a legal background to understand it? Write the definitions in plain English, for everyone to understand.

❖ As with any other document, check for loopholes. Better yet, share the document with others before submitting it. Loopholes are like typos—they're next to impossible to see yourself.

Finding Forms

The forms never stop coming in the life of the corporation paralegal. Here are some tips on good ways to locate them:

❖ Every secretary of state has a Web site, and, on most of those Web sites, you can link to the forms you need for your filings, depending on whether you're organizing, merging, consolidating, or dissolving your business entities. But some of those Web sites are a bit maze-like and you'll find that some states charge for forms whereas others don't. If you're in a pinch, or have the money to spend, you could log on to http://www.ctadvantage.com, which is the Web site for CT Corporation System, which has all the forms you'll need for any state. They're all free for subscribers, so if you have a volume in this kind of work, it may pay for you to subscribe to this kind of service.

❖ A resource we all should know about is http://www.nass.org, which is the Web site of the National Association of Secretaries of State. Every secretary of state in the Union is here and you'll find most of the forms you'll ever need this way.

❖ When you're looking for standard letters and forms relevant to federal trademark filings, make a visit to the International Trademark Association at http://www.inta.org or the U.S. Patent and Trademark Office at http://www.uspto.gov. Between the two of them, they'll have everything you need.

Closings

One of your duties as a corporate paralegal may be to preside over closings. These can go smoothly or not so smoothly, depending on how you run things.

❖ Somebody's got to be the traffic cop in the closing room, and that's you. Even though you may not be as major a player as some of the people you're dealing with, as long as you conduct yourself with confidence, dignity, and a no-nonsense approach, you shouldn't have a problem maintaining order and flow.

❖ When money or property changes hands, some people can get kind of hyped up and obnoxious. Don't take any flak from anyone. Nicely but firmly assert yourself.

❖ Make sure you have extra closing agendas on hand for anyone who happens to drop in. Sometimes people arrive at a closing with a retinue.

❖ Papers arrive in folders and leave in folders. Never break that rule!

❖ All items on the closing agenda should be numbered and the numbers should be shown on the folder labels. That way you can easily keep everything in order.

❖ I use different colored post-its on documents, with each color representing a signer. As the documents are signed, I peel off the post-it.

QUICK TIPS FOR PARALEGALS OF ALL DIFFERENT STRIPES

There are so many avenues of employment for paralegals that we will only offer a very quick overview of these other areas along with a tip or two.

Family Law

Here paralegals are involved in family matters, such as marriage, divorce, alimony, child support, and child custody.

❖ I was a social worker, but got burned out on it. I knew I wanted to do something in the area of children and the law, so I became a family-law paralegal. Then I went to work for an attorney who specializes in adoption. I couldn't be happier. Every day that I go to work, I feel like I'm helping to make miracles happen.

❖ Divorce is an incredibly stressful experience, and working on a daily basis with people going through a divorce is no picnic. I have a lot of people crying on my shoulder, which is okay with me—I'm basically a naturally empathetic person—but if you're not that kind of person, find another area to work in.

❖ When you're working in the area of family law, it's sometimes hard to keep yourself from being seen not only as a paralegal, but as a counselor, a confessor, and someone who can be called on to do a little of everything. I feel a lot of the pain of the people I work with, especially the abused women, but my billable hours don't cover activities like teaching someone how to balance a checkbook after their husband's walked out on them. So I've made up a master book of resources that our clients can refer to. I've got reputable debt consolidation agencies in there and Consumer Credit Card Counseling and emergency food and shelter hotline numbers and community pro bono legal services if their money runs out or if it looks like it just isn't there in the first place and Child Protection Services and lots more. It saves the client and me a lot of frustration this way.

❖ Working in this area usually means having a lot of contact with mediators. I have a girlfriend who's a family law paralegal like me, and she trained to become a mediator. It's something I think about doing when my kids get older and my life is a little less crazed.

Bankruptcy Law

Your duties here will include interviewing debtors; obtaining information regarding their income, debts and assets; reviewing the claims of creditors and verifying their validity; and preparing documents for bankruptcy court and attending proceedings.

❖ There is a lot of stress in doing this work. You are involved with people who are really on the ropes and the burnout factor for you can be high. On the other hand, as with any situation where you are helping people in need, there can be a great deal of satisfaction in the work as well. You have to find the balance.

Trusts and Estates

A paralegal in this area will be interviewing clients to determine their assets, how they wish to have these assets assigned upon their death, and what arrangements they wish to make for guardianship of their minor children. You will be involved in the drafting of wills and documents relating to trust funds. You will file documents required by probate, and will explain the probate process to family members and heirs. You may also be involved in locating heirs.

❖ Continuing education is an absolute must in this area. Federal and state tax laws change constantly, and you have to stay abreast and afloat.

❖ The way I see it, Trusts and Estates is a little bit about a lot of things. You need to know aspects of real estate law, corporate law, family law, maybe even litigation. That's what makes it so interesting!

❖ Keep in mind that you're going to be working with people who have suffered loss. There are a lot of emotional needs in this picture. You will be dealing with elderly widows or widowers who require patience and kindness. You may be dealing with angry people who feel left out of the will, which requires other people skills from you. It can be demanding, but it can also be very interesting and ultimately gratifying.

❖ If you're in T & E, you really have to check into the case management programs that are available. In the past, these programs were mostly in place only for litigation practices, but now we've got them too and they make life so much easier. Amicus Attorney, Jr. Partner, and Time Matters are some of the programs that people are using. Do your networking and see which one sounds best for you.

Real Estate Law

This lively and complex area of law will have you interviewing buyers and sellers, working up sales contracts, conducting title examinations, reviewing title abstracts, drafting mortgage agreements, preparing deeds, scheduling and perhaps attending closings, and more.

❖ I think real estate is just in certain people's blood. I love it. I love everything about it. Little houses, big houses . . . it doesn't matter. To me, it's just fascinating to watch property change hands.

❖ As you can imagine, there are countless details that come into play around a real estate transaction and here, perhaps even more than in many other areas of law, the paralegal picks up the slack to such a degree that I often find I develop more of a relationship with the client than I did when I worked as a paralegal in other areas of law.

❖ Generally, a real estate transaction goes according to form. There are definite steps and signposts along the way. So a paralegal should be totally familiar with the process and should be able to anticipate and red-light anything that comes up that threatens to derail that well-worn process.

❖ Your volume of calls as a real estate paralegal can be huge. You're calling buyers, sellers, attorneys, title search people, surveyors . . . you name it. Just make sure you keep an extra-careful phone log, so you know what calls you've made, what calls you have to make, who has gotten back to you, and who hasn't.

Immigration Law

One of the fastest-growing specialty areas is immigration law. As a paralegal in this area, you will assist clients with obtaining work permits and visas, and you will help them with their citizenship process. You may also be involved in helping clients who are faced with deportation.

❖ If you want some drama in your life, head for immigration. It can be very stressful, but it also can make you feel incredibly good when you've helped someone in desperate straits. I also find it fascinating to meet people from so many different cultures. It's been a real education for me.

❖ Immigration law changes fast. I log in with the State Department on an almost daily basis (http://www.state. gov). Immigration Lawyers on the Internet is another excellent site http://www.ilw.com).

❖ Immigration law is very intricate and detail-oriented. You have to be a highly thorough person to do well in this area. I keep checklists of everything.

❖ As an immigration paralegal, you'll find it particularly important and useful to network with other paralegals in your area. A lot of jobs that might be possibilities for your clients come about through word-of-mouth. Your fellow immigration paralegals can also recommend to you good passport/visa service companies.

❖ If ever there was an area where you needed some good "tickling," immigration is it. Your clients, understandably, are extremely antsy about the progress of their cases. I routinely send out update notices as to their status, and, as they've come to understand what they'll be getting from me and when, it cuts down on the frantic phone calls.

There are other fascinating areas of law for the paralegal to explore—elder law, environmental law, criminal law, employment and labor law, personal-injury law, intellectual-property—but in the remainder of the space we have allotted for this chapter, we'd like to look at one last area for paralegals to think about: a freelance, or independent, paralegal practice.

FREELANCE PARALEGALS

Increasingly, many paralegals are opting to become freelance paralegals, also known as independent or contract paralegals. In this capacity, a paralegal owns his or her own business and performs certain specific types of legal tasks for attorneys on a contract basis.

❖ I became a freelancer because I wanted to have more control over my time. My husband died and my kids needed me to be at home. Fortunately, I had insurance money so I had something to cushion me from the terror of being totally on my own financially. But I didn't feel like I had a lot of choice. I needed to be at home more—that's just the way it was.

❖ Why did I do it? Because I saw friends of mine who were making just as good or better money without having to deal with a boss hanging over them every day. Believe me, my boss was not somebody you'd want hanging over you every day . . . or even every other day. So it's had its rough patches, this independent life, but, on a day-to-day basis, I'm happy with it.

❖ I did it because I realized that the one thing I really loved to do in my job as a paralegal was the research. And I'm great at that. So now I do legal research for a handful of attorneys, and that's all I do. I don't have to do any of the other stuff I never liked to do.

❖ I did it because the attorney I was working for couldn't afford to have me full-time anymore. The economic downturns meant that he wasn't exactly cleaning up in accounts receivable so he had to make cuts. I live in a small city in New Hampshire, and there were a number of attorneys in the same situation as the one that I had been working for, so I managed to put together a group of them for whom I now work on a freelance basis. Do

I like it better? Well, it's a challenge and I can't say I love paying for my own medical insurance, but I do get a certain sense of pride and satisfaction in running my own business. I never thought I would, but here I am, keeping my head above water. That certainly counts for something, doesn't it?

❖ I tell people to figure on start-up costs of about five grand. As a freelance paralegal, you'll need to spend about $2,000 on a computer, maybe another thousand on basic software, about a thousand on your fax, printer, and phone, and then maybe $1,500 on furniture, supplies, and books. That's not the moon, folks.

❖ A lot of people have this fantasy about working for yourself. The flip side of the fantasy is the bad dream. What if you get sick? What if business goes bye-bye? What about the isolation? What about promoting your business? I don't want to rain on anybody's parade, and I do think freelancing can be great for some people. You just have to know who you are.

❖ What's the number one thing you need to make it as freelance paralegal? Forget the office location, forget the contacts, forget the Chamber of Commerce. It's the discipline. Can you get yourself to work every day or does it just seem too beautiful out not to take that bike ride? That's the rub.

❖ It seems obvious, but I might as well say it. Don't go and become a freelance paralegal before you've had a lot of experience working in a law firm. You won't get the supervision you need and your clients obviously aren't going to walk you through your paces.

❖ Why go cold turkey and start your freelance business by leaving your job and hanging up a shingle? I started my freelancing while I was still in a regular job, doing law tasks at night at home for friends, neighbors, and so forth. You've got to make sure you're not involved in any conflict-of-interest activities, but it's a good way to begin.

❖ By all means, if you're freelancing, you need to network more than ever. You could start with your local paralegal association. They might keep a file of freelancers and will be happy to add your name to it.

❖ I wouldn't even think about becoming a freelance para-legal if I lived somewhere that didn't have a high-speed Internet connection. Can you imagine doing legal research without it?

❖ For me, the biggest headache in going freelance was fig-uring out what to charge. Now that I have more experi-ence, I would advise those new to freelancing to network with other freelancers to find out what the going rate is. You might want to charge on a project basis rather than an hourly basis.

❖ When you take on a client, be sure to ask them what their billing cycle is. You should always note something like "Payment due within 30 days" on your invoice, but, after a conversation with a client, you may realize that realistically you should not expect payment within such a time frame and you should make the necessary adjustments to your cash-flow expectations.

❖ Some people like to do business with a handshake, while others want a letter of agreement. You can find samples of letters of agreement in the forms books pub-lished within your state.

❖ I think it's more important than ever as a freelance para-legal to get your assignments in writing. Deadlines and a rough estimate of the time expected to complete the project should be included.

❖ Make sure your formatting is in synch with your clients. As you probably know, all firms have their own little formatting peculiarities.

❖ If you thought that insane deadlines would no longer be part of your life when you turned to freelancing, think again. Freelancers seem to often be the ones called in to bail people out at the last minute, and dead-lines can be excruciating.

❖ If you have a long-term freelance relationship with a firm, make sure you get into their office now and then. Stop by and deliver something. If you're never actually seen, it's hard for people to relate to you as a real human being.

❖ Marketing yourself is a big concern for freelancers. You may want to check out a marketing firm, or perhaps barter your services with someone who has expertise in that area. Marketing yourself can also be a less formal, more intimate experience. You can send holiday cards or drop by with a basket of mini-muffins or whatever for a good client. Nobody minds a little special attention.

❖ When you're working for yourself, and you've got nobody giving you perks like free tuition to educational seminars, your continuing legal education can be a challenge. Then again, when you work for yourself, CLE is more important than ever, because you're not going to hear about important changes in the law at the water cooler. What I do is I read a lot of journals, and I have my own encyclopedia that I'm always adding to. It's got sections like Witnesses or Evidence or Web Sites or Personal Injury and I'll clip anything that looks interesting from the journals and paste it into the relevant section of the encyclopedia. It's really quite something!

❖ Freelancing is not a busman's holiday by any means. It can be even more demanding than being a full-time paralegal in an office. You've got to be able to make time for yourself and your family during which you put down the work. You've got to remember to go on vacation, which can be hard to do when nobody's paying you for one. It's great to be able to carve out some dedicated office space too in your home, rather than turning your bedroom, let's say, into a partial office.

❖ Be really up on UPL issues. They're a particular matter of concern to freelance paralegals.

❖ When it comes to taxes, my advice is to invest in a bookkeeper or an accountant. Don't try to do it all yourself. You won't succeed.

War Stories:

. . . And Still More Procrastination

I had to sometimes work with an attorney who always did things at the last minute, say 4:58 (my work schedule was 8:00 A.M. to 5 P.M). What I would be given would, naturally, have to be done immediately because the attorney wanted it back the next morning by 8:00 A.M. The work was usually lengthy and would typically take about two hours to complete.

I tried to get around this problem by having the secretaries forward me the docket (fortunately, I was in good with them!). If I got the docket before it was distributed to the attorneys, I would know what cases would hit me in advance and I could get a jump on them by getting the "routine" documents needed. Then I would drop into the attorney's office during the day to ask if he needed any assistance with his case. He would think I was being oh-so-helpful, and I guess I was, but in reality I was trying to avoid having all the work fall on me at the last minute.

In order for the above to work, a paralegal must practice the art of gentle and professional assertiveness and take initiative. You have to be knowledgeable and be absolutely positive that you know what you're doing: getting the deadlines, implementing the work on a priority basis according to your deadline, returning it for review, following it up to get it back pronto, and so on. It will work to your benefit to become knowledgeable about your firm's cases so that you can stay one step ahead of your attorney. Attorneys may know their stuff in court, but a lot of them can be very disorganized with their paperwork!

CHAPTER 10

The Savvy Paralegal

Speaking of "survival"—for that, after all, is the word that features in the title of this book—we should all recognize that if we are to survive in today's work world, we need to be flexible, forward-thinking, and proactive about our careers. Resting on our laurels is never an option. If the job you're in no longer feels right, then it is time to consider change. Inertia is anathema to success.

No matter how many times you've been through the job-hunting search, each time has its own set of anxieties attached to it. It is not a fun process, but keep in mind that it can be a highly rewarding one. Like everything else in life, job-hunting relies on a set of skills and when you learn these skills and hone them, you will always feel empowered to be in control of your career.

An important aspect of job-hunting has to do with networking: connecting with and listening to other people. Think of this chapter then as an exercise in networking. You will be hearing from others in the field who have shared your aspirations and your difficulties and who have found useful and creative ways to approach the job of job-hunting.

LAYING THE GROUNDWORK

Is the right job out there waiting for you? The only way to find out is to start looking. Don't let yourself languish in a work situation where you feel overworked, undervalued, and underpaid. But, before you hit the street, do a self-check to see how ready you are.

❖ It's critical to take a proactive stance when it comes to finding a job. Don't wait for someone to tap you on the shoulder—for most of us, that doesn't usually happen. When you do decide to look for a job, kick off the process by conducting a "review" of yourself. You need to have a good grasp of just how valuable you would be to a potential employer.

❖ Before I'd even consider making a job change, I'd want to make sure I was working up to my full potential. To determine whether I was or not, I would give myself a critique and a "grade." Over the years, I've developed a list of criteria—my attitude (is it positive enough?); my appearance (is it professional?); punctuality; continuing education; my teamwork skills—and I would really give some hard thought as to how well I was doing. If I weren't sure, I'd ask someone I trust to help critique me. When I felt that I'd gotten my "grades" up to an "A" level, then I'd feel that I was ready to look for a job.

❖ It always amazes me how many people stay in dead-end jobs. And it's not because that's the easy way out—usually these jobs have some really serious drawbacks and there's nothing easy about feeling frustrated and disappointed. I think the reason so many people allow themselves to be undervalued has to do with self-image and motivation. So, in some cases, the job hunt really has to begin with taking a hard look at yourself and maybe even seeking some intervention from a counselor or a psychotherapist if you think your self-esteem and motivation need work.

❖ Whenever I'm contemplating a job change, I ask myself a series of questions. What's my passion? What's my peeve? What am I good at? Do I want more or less responsibility? Where do I want to be in a year? In five years? If I don't ask myself these questions, then I don't come up with any answers.

❖ Assessing the job you're in should be an ongoing activity. Just as you are slated for a performance review once a year or once every six months, so should you subject your job to a review. Sometimes you get so caught up in the work that you can't achieve perspective and you stay in a job even if it's not what you really want. That's called a rut.

❖ We all hear a lot about "dream jobs." Mostly, it's a bunch of hooey. To me, dream jobs are like dream families: no one I know has one. All jobs come with their problems, and usually the problems are too much or too little work, crazy people, long commutes, no room for advancement or any and all of the above.

LEAVING YOUR LAWYER

Leaving the people you work for does not have to be a Shakespearean tragedy. It happens all the time; in fact, it's the way of the world. In other words, there's a right way to do it and a wrong way to do it, and you want to do it the right way.

❖ Generally speaking, there's no reason why you shouldn't be able to walk out that door with a good feeling and references intact. One reason why it might not work out that way is because too much free-floating emotion gets unleashed. Sometimes people who have been working together for a long time think of their relationship as a kind of marriage. Well, guess what? It isn't! You never got the ring; you never said the vows. So when you feel like it's time to move on, because you want more money or better work conditions or are simply in the mood for a change, go about it with a mature and worldly air that lets your employers know that you, and they, should take this all in stride.

❖ Turn the other cheek. Then turn another one still. If you run out of cheeks, borrow one. Your assignment, if you should choose to accept it and you really should choose to accept it if you have any brains, is to walk out of that door without enemies. The legal world is much too small for enemies.

❖ You may have to do some long-range planning before you leave the job you're in. You might want to give yourself a year's notice, during which time you upgrade your skills to make sure that you are fully marketable. How are you on the computer? Is your Internet acumen up to snuff? How many specialties can you claim any knowledge of or experience in? Be frank with yourself. Don't try to fool yourself and don't try to fool other people. In the long run, nobody's fooled.

❖ I'm sure everybody's heard this from his or her father, mother, uncle, and aunt, but it's good advice no matter how many times you've heard it. Don't leave a job until you've got a job. End of story.

❖ Never give less than two weeks notice, no matter how much of a strain your current position may be. Never give more than four weeks notice. Your current employer may find diabolical ways to torture you in such a generous time frame and your new employer may get tired of waiting for you to arrive.

❖ If you should happen to get a counter-offer from your present employer, ask yourself if your desire for change is simply about the money or whether it's real and broad-based.

❖ Your last few weeks in a job should be not only about training your successor, but about cementing the ties to the people you've enjoyed working with. Take a valued colleague out to lunch. Write thank-you notes to anyone who's been helpful to you over the years. Be sentimental. No one will object.

❖ Be as generous as you can be with training your successor. That person is just another person for you to network with down the road. If you've been generous to her, she'll always remember. If you've been remote or uninterested, she'll always remember.

❖ You have to be careful about what kinds of files you can take with you, but I always manage to spirit out any kind of letters or other communications that have mentioned what a good job I've done. That's my insurance for the future.

❖ I go on a cleaning binge when I leave a job. I transmute into Mr. Wizard. You could eat off my desk, my floor, my file cabinets. I might even buy a plant for the new person coming in.

Continuing Education

It is a fact of life as a paralegal. Here are some good ideas about how to go about it:

- Most local and state chapters of the National Association of Legal Assistants and the National Federation of Paralegal Associations offer a wealth of professional seminars.
- Enrolling in a night class at a college or university might be an exciting and productive experience, but have a thorough conversation with the Admissions Department first to make sure that the course content is what you're looking for.
- State or local bar associations often open their classes to paralegals.
- An advantage of a large law firm is that you may be able to take courses offered in-house by attorneys and paralegal managers.
- Check out online opportunities for CLE, but then network to make sure that the choices are good ones.

❖ Nothing's tackier than one of those midnight raids when you stuff shopping bags with file cards, Rolodexes, staplers, and anything else you can get your hands on. You've got a good new job. Would you rather spend the next few years in Sing-Sing?

RETRAINING

Retraining—that is, learning a new area of law—may become necessary if you're thinking of switching jobs or even if you're staying in your current job, depending upon any changes in your current employer's situation.

❖ More and more, law firms and corporate law departments are looking for individuals who can multi-task. You need diverse skills in this climate. That means continuing education and retraining as necessary.

❖ If you're a paralegal, you have to get used to the idea of change. Change is built into this profession. The law is an ever-changing organism, and we need to keep up with it. I've gotten myself to the point where instead of being afraid of change, I feel excited (and a little scared) about it.

❖ Before I would make a change, I'd network as much as I could with people in that area to see if it sounded like it was for me. That's called research, which is what we paralegals are supposed to be good at!

❖ If you just feel like you need "a change" in your life, ask yourself if that change has to be in your professional orbit. Maybe you're just in a blah phase and taking up a new hobby would satisfy your desire for change. Learning ballroom dancing, for instance. That could be a lot easier and more fun than changing from maritime law to trusts and estates, no?

❖ Retraining is one thing; continuing education is another. As paralegals, we should always be out there, brushing up our education. If this leads us to want to make a major change, so be it. But it doesn't necessarily have to mean that.

REGARDING RÉSUMÉS

If there's one thing most paralegals are comfortable with, it's forms. That should be good news for paralegal job hunters, for the résumé, the basic tool one uses in a job search, is essentially just another kind of form. But, like the shoemaker whose shoes are rundown, the paralegal who is so good at handling forms may not be so good when those forms strike close to home. Crafting a powerful résumé is extremely important, for it is the written summary of your education and work experience and will tell potential employers at a glance all about your achievements and accomplishments. Here are some thoughts from your colleagues on the subject of résumés.

❖ Rule Number One: Keep it short. One page. Nothing more. Unless you're a Nobel Prize-winning physicist with 30 books to your credit, one page should be plenty.

❖ The operative word is "simplicity." Leave off folders, attachments, writing samples. Just the facts, Ma'am.

❖ No photos, please. That makes your résumé look like the kind of MOST WANTED notice you'd find in the post office.

❖ I use the phrase "references on request." To actually list references on your résumé has, to me, a less-than-professional feeling.

❖ Make sure you put your résumé on good-quality paper that is white, buff, or gray.

❖ When it comes to résumés, there's a big argument over how to order the listing of your achievements. Check with library sources or on the Internet for format. Some people like to arrange the résumé by chronologically listing positions held. Other people prefer to arrange it by functions performed. You'll have to check it out and decide for yourself.

❖ Use dates. Some people, to avoid whatever gaps they may have, leave off dates, but most employers really do want to see dates.

❖ When listing your accomplishments, be as specific as you can. Take an inventory before you even sit down to do your résumé so that you have a clear view of what it is you've actually accomplished. Any good résumé-writing resource will have a list of "action" words that you can draw upon to describe the work you've done. These words include such winners as "troubleshooting," "problem-solving," "coordinating," "researching," "analyzing," "budgeting," "policy-making," and so on.

❖ Don't forget to list any honors and awards you've received and make sure to include memberships in any professional organizations.

❖ List all of your continuing education courses!

❖ Don't forget that people are busy, so make your pitch clear and concise. Don't use long, elaborate sentences that wish to extol the magnificence and munificence of your grand and distinguished career. Keep it simple and straightforward.

❖ Proofread, my friends, proofread. Misspellings and poor grammar will mean points taken off. And in this competitive job market, you can't afford to lose points on stuff like that. Just ask a friend or family member to give your résumé the once-over. But make sure that person is a decent proofreader.

❖ Be consistent with your formatting and styling. If you use bold or italics in one situation, carry it through.

❖ Nothing, nothing, nothing goes into the résumé about your salary requirements. Any talk about salary is restricted to your interview, and only if and when the interviewer brings the subject up.

❖ If nothing else, remember this rule: *never ever* lie on your résumé. It will come back to haunt you, and, when the grapevine gets a hold of what you've done, you might have some really serious problems finding a job in the town you live in.

❖ Some résumé reference sources will tell you to list personal interests, like hobbies or the fact that you're a member of the National Audubon Society or whatever. I've never cared for that on a résumé. Frankly, I just don't find it very relevant.

Cover Letters

Just as important as the résumé is the cover letter. If a prospective employer is not favorably impressed with the cover letter, he or she may never even get to the résumé.

❖ Rule Number One: Make sure your contact information is on your cover letter. It's not good enough just to have it on your résumé.

❖ Spend as much time and creative energy as necessary to develop an interesting first sentence. The cover letter is your first impression, even more than the résumé, and that first sentence is your "first" first impression.

❖ Customize your cover letter for each job you go for. Don't try to get away with a "form" letter, simply changing the head each time you send it somewhere. You have to make the recipient feel like you're going for *that* job in *that* firm.

❖ Once again, simplicity is the rule. Keep it short and sweet. Don't tell them your life story.

❖ List a few key skills. Of course, they'll be listed in your résumé as well, but having them in the cover letter is a kind of preview to whet the employer's interest.

NETWORKING

Some people manage to find jobs through the classifieds, the Internet, or through job search firms, but many of the best jobs are never advertised and the way to get at them is through networking.

❖ Networking is just an outgrowth of human nature. People want to help people. Why? Because they think that you may help them or their wives or sons or daughters or nieces or nephews down the road. That's the driving force behind it.

❖ I read somewhere that public speaking is the most widespread fear. Right on its heels, I would wager, is the kind of mingling with strangers that goes on at networking cocktail parties and such. I can remember how much that terrified me, but the way I got over it was by practicing with people outside of my work world. I'm a shy person, but I gave myself the assignment of striking up a conversation with some parent I didn't know sitting next to me on the bleachers at a Little League game, or with somebody on the elevator in my apartment building. With these kinds of social interactions under my belt, I felt more secure about going up to strangers at networking events and making small talk.

❖ Learning to mingle is a skill that, like any other skill, will improve the more you practice. Don't get stuck with just one person at a networking event. That's not what it's for. Be friendly and introduce yourself to a lot of people. If you come across a cold fish, don't take it personally. They're not playing the game as it was meant to be played, but you are!

❖ Always collect business cards when you've been networking and write down on the back of the card a note or two about the encounter.

❖ Test your wings around public speaking by volunteering for something like a career day at your local high school. If you've handled that okay, you might want to work your way up to seminars or speaking at bar meetings regarding subjects of concern for paralegals.

❖ Start making yourself known in your profession. Join professional organizations and become active in them. There's no better way to network.

❖ Don't abuse the connections you make through networking. For instance, I would never ask a relative stranger for a reference, or drop somebody's name if I don't know that person well.

❖ One thing I can't stand is when I'm talking to somebody at one of these networking events and we may be talking about a movie that's out or the new Mexican restaurant in town and all of a sudden I'm being hit up for a job lead. That kind of transition, or lack of it, drives me crazy.

❖ If you've made an appointment with somebody and have asked for fifteen minutes of his time, don't ask for more than that. Fifteen minutes is fifteen minutes.

❖ Every now and then, your networking overtures may lead to a door being slammed in your face. If so, just suck it up. There are people in the world who simply aren't very nice or very helpful or very sympathetic. Don't turn the behavior of these people into a personal rejection.

❖ A sincere "thank you" counts for a great deal. If someone has helped you, by answering questions over the phone or by meeting with you, make sure you follow up their act of kindness with your own. A brief note of thanks will stamp you in that person's memory as someone who knows how to do the right thing.

❖ Help others as much as you can. I'm really of the belief that when you help others, your good deeds come back to you.

THE ALL-IMPORTANT INTERVIEW

The résumé and networking are designed to get your foot in the door. So now that you've got that foot in the door, what's your next step?

❖ First impressions count for a lot. That's just the way the world works. Think of how you've felt on occasions when a blind date comes to your door. Well, when you go into an interview, you're the blind date. That means that your grooming and your wardrobe have to be impeccable.

❖ I'll let you in on a secret: some people *hate* perfume. So why risk it? Leave the Chanel No. 5 home that day.

❖ Carry a handbag or a briefcase—never both. You don't want to look like you're moving in on the poor guy.

❖ Bring an extra copy of your résumé to the interview. Even if you've already sent one, the interviewer may not have it at her fingertips, so why be caught short?

❖ Research the firm before you arrive for the interview. It helps you to frame intelligent questions.

❖ Anticipate questions. Obviously, you know that certain ones are going to come up. *Why did you leave your last job? Why do you want to work here?* You need to do your homework and make sure you've got some good responses handy.

❖ I've compiled a list of good questions to ask at an interview. Things like: Are there plans for growth in this department over the next year? How can a responsible legal assistant grow professionally here? How many billable hours are required? Is this a new position? If it's not, then why did the last paralegal leave? Can I speak with another paralegal in the group? Some of these questions may sound a bit shocking, but going into a job is a big commitment and you should be entitled to ask the questions that you want answers to.

❖ Role-playing your interview with friends or family can be very useful. Just make sure you're doing it with someone who knows how to be a serious critic.

❖ Punctuality is the number one rule. Never, ever, be late for an interview. Assume that if you're late, even by one minute, you've lost that job.

❖ To make sure I don't show up late for an interview, I scout out the location a day in advance. Even if it's an hour away, I make the trip and check the address. I go right up to the door so that I'm not wandering around the next day, in a sweat, in some office park two minutes before I'm due for the actual interview.

❖ Smile. When you walk in the door, when you leave, and whenever you can in-between. A good smile is one of the best tools in your tool shed.

❖ Never lean on or touch an interviewer's desk or place your things on the desk. Some people are very territorial about their desks and you might get marks against you for this.

❖ I have actually heard of people walking into an interview with a cup of coffee or who have chewed gum during an interview. Guess whether they got the job or not.

❖ Sit up straight and speak clearly, just like your mother used to tell you to.

❖ Whatever you do, do not criticize your past employers. An interview is not an occasion for you to air gripes. You'll only come off sounding like a malcontent or a loose canon.

❖ Always shake the hand of your interviewer at the end and say thank you for his or her time.

❖ Don't talk about money in the interview. There's a time and a place for that. If somehow it can't be avoided, don't quote any figures that you'll then be wed to. Say something like, "If you think I'm right for this job, I would entertain your best offer."

❖ Don't forget to follow up your interview with a thank-you note. It's required. And it will give you the opportunity to restate your eagerness to fill the position, which could wind up being a key factor if the interviewer is choosing between two or three people.

❖ Keep in mind that there are certain questions that an interviewer does not have the right to ask and that you do not have to answer. Anything having to do with your race, religion, national origin or citizenship, age, marital status, sexual preference, disabilities, physical traits . . . these are all off-limits. If one of these questions comes up, you should politely but firmly state that you do not think the question is relevant to the position being filled and that you would like to focus on those qualities and attributes that are relevant. The message should sink in and your interviewer may actually wind up being impressed with your presence of mind.

SALARY NEGOTIATIONS

For some people, talking about money is painful. It doesn't have to be. Here are some good tips on negotiating money.

❖ Do your homework. Know what the going rate is for the position being filled. The more information you have, the more powerful your negotiating position will be.

❖ Negotiating for a job is not like negotiating for a car. If the negotiations work out, you and the person you're negotiating with are going to be living with each other, so operate out of good will. Don't assume an adversarial position, as if the person you're negotiating with is a rug merchant in a Turkish bazaar, out to get you. Also, it helps to realize that if you're being offered the position, that means that the firm you're negotiating with has made up its mind that you're the one for the job and so you both have the same goal: to make this happen.

❖ There are a lot of "extras" that may factor into your total package. Be aware of what they are. It could be vacation time, continuing education, flex time, a six-month review with performance increases. Look into all of these and whatever else you can creatively come up with and keep them in mind when you're making your deal.

❖ Never lie. Don't say you made more than you actually did on your last job. On the other hand, you don't have to show all your cards. In a way, a salary negotiation is a little like a game of poker . . . a bit of bluffing, the old poker face. Maybe your first time out doing it, it will not go so well. But, with practice, you may wind up winning a few hands.

❖ Make "fairness" the operative word in the negotiations. If cost of living has gone up, then it is only fair that your wages should rise accordingly. If your employer has budgetary restraints due to a slow economy, it is only fair that you take that into account.

❖ Bargaining is expected, but there comes a time when you run the risk of overkill. When you feel the offer is in the zone, then back off. Don't hold on for every last penny. Even if your demands are met, your employer may walk away from the experience feeling that he has hired a prima donna. Remember that negotiation is about give-and-take all around.

Keep in mind, at all times, that you have chosen a terrific field and the opportunities for job satisfaction are out there. Good Luck!

INDEX

A

absent-minded boss, 11
alcoholic as boss, 11
American Medical Forensic
    Specialists, 130
analytical skills, 3
asking questions, in
    communication, 25
assertiveness, 26, 37
Association of Scientific
    Advisors, 130
attitude, interpersonal skills
    and, 26–29

B

backing up computer files, 114
backpacks, 55
bankruptcy law, 145
benefit packages, 139
billable hours, 63–64, 91–93
biorhythms, 64
body language and
    expressions, 23
boredom, 4
briefcases and backpacks,
    55

C

calendaring, in litigation law,
    121–122
case law research, 101–102
case management systems
    (CMS), 116
citation checking, 101

closings, 143–144
code of behavior, 71
color coding for organization,
    90–91
communication basics, 23–26
    asking questions, 25
    body language and
        expressions in, 23
    e-mail and, 116–118
    listening skills in, 24–25
    mirroring technique in, 25
    paying attention in, 24
    space barriers in, 23
    stress relief through, 48–49
    telephone courtesy and, 39,
        125
    voice used in, 24
computer skills, 3
confidentiality, 73–75
conflict resolution, 31–34
    in salary negotiation, 164–165
continuing education, 6, 61–63,
    156–157
Corporate Focus, Two Step
    Software, 142
corporate paralegals, 3, 135–141
    closings and, 143–144
    form finding for, 143
    minute books for, 141–142
    reviewing corporate policies
        for, 142–143
cover letters for resumes,
    159–160
creativity, 4, 7–8